ROUGH MUSIC

Blair / Bombs / Baghdad / London / Terror

TARIQ ALI

VERSO

London • New York

First published by Verso 2005
This edition published by Verso 2005
© Tariq Ali 2005

All rights reserved

The moral rights of the author have been asserted

1 3 5 7 9 10 8 6 4 2

Verso
UK: 6 Meard Street, London WIF OEG
USA: 180 Varick Street, New York, NY 10014–4606
www.versobooks.com

Verso is the imprint of New Left Books

ISBN 1–84467–545–9

British Library Cataloguing in Publication Data
A catalogue record for this book is available from the British
Library

Library of Congress Cataloging-in-Publication Data
A catalog record for this book is available from the Library of
Congress

Typeset in Sabon by New Left Review

Printed and Bound in the UK
by Cox & Wyman Ltd, Reading, Berkshire

In memory of Paul Foot
greatly missed in these scoundrel times

CONTENTS

APPENDICES

1

What Makes Blair Run

ON 7 JULY 2005, the murderous chaos of Blair's war in Iraq came home to London in a lethal series of suicide bombings. Two weeks later, with apparent impunity, security forces shot dead Jean Charles de Menezes, a young Brazilian electrician on his way to work. The terror attacks in London, and the descent into apparently endless war in the Middle East that sparked them, have marked a watershed in British political culture. How many of the Labour voters celebrating victory on that beautiful spring morning in May 1997 anticipated that it would come to this?

New Labour's socio-economic trajectory had been more predictable. The plan had been laid out with bullet point clarity in *The Blair Revolution*, put out by Peter Mandelson and Roger Liddle in 1996: the free-market Thatcherite model would be maintained, ameliorated by a few low-cost anti-poverty measures. The revolution of 'choice' would be pushed through the health and education services. The criminal justice system would be toughened. In 1994 I had predicted in the *New Statesman* that the Blair project was to transform Labour into a British version of the Democratic Party. Shortly after the 1997 victory, Blair suggested that it was time that 'elections fought on the basis of ideology and politics' were brought to an end.

This was not a case of betrayal; if anything had been betrayed it was the illusions others had about him. Blair never claimed to be a supporter of Nye Bevan or Anthony Crosland. A year or so before the Tory defeat, reviewing Sir Geoffrey Howe's memoirs in the *Financial Times*, Nigel Lawson concluded: 'Mrs Thatcher's true successor is currently Leader of the Opposition'. Nevertheless, the talk of 'no politics' and 'no ideology' was nonsense. In his first days in office Gordon Brown had sent a clear message to the City by handing command over interest rates to the Bank of England: don't worry, be happy. As Seumas Milne pointed out, in one of the sharpest and most prescient critiques of the Blair project (published while much of the country was giddy with euphoria), there was a very clear political goal:

> Within three weeks of the Party's election victory, four prominent businessmen had been appointed or approached to join or advise the Government: Sir David Simon, Chairman of BP, to become European Competition Minister, Martin Taylor, chief executive of Barclays Bank, to lead a Whitehall task force on tax and benefits, Lord Hollick, chairman of United News and Media, to advise on industrial policy, and Peter Jarvis, Whitbread Chief Executive, who was asked to head the Low Pay Commission, charged with setting the rate for the planned legal wage . . .
>
> There is no question that the crowning of New Labour represents a historic break . . . For the New Labour advance guard—Blair, Peter Mandelson and their closest supporters—that means an unconditional embrace of the new rules of the globalised economic game, with its privatized, deregulated, free-fire zones for

multinational business, along with the new balance of power that goes with it, both at home and abroad.[1]

Blair's hyper-militarism was not so easy to foresee—though there was a premonition of it in the whipping of the Labour Shadow Cabinet to produce unanimous support for Clinton and Major's 1996 air strikes on Iraq. In office, Blair's first blooding was again in the skies over Iraq: Operation Desert Fox, unleashed in December 1998 as Clinton faced impeachment charges, blasted a hundred targets in southern Iraq over the course of seventy hours; it was just the start of the bombing campaign that would continue more or less uninterrupted until Operation Iraqi Freedom.

Mere months later, in the spring of 1999, Blair would be baying for a full-scale military invasion of Yugoslavia. At this point it became clear that Blair was excited by war. He liked being surrounded by military men. He liked the smell of blood. But the driving force was political. I am often asked by anti-war activists—leftists and liberals in the United States especially—what explains Tony Blair. How can a Labour Prime Minister adopt the position of a neo-conservative Bushite so rapidly, and with such fervent conviction? Is there a psychological explanation? Is it religion?

My response is that though character and religion may play a part, the answer lies in politics. Like any

---

[1] Seumas Milne, 'After the May Day Flood', *London Review of Books*, 5 June 1997. This hard-headed realism has certainly passed the test of time. *New Left Review,* the magazine with which I am associated, was much more emollient at the time.

3

latter-day British premier, Blair believes in the dogmas of the Washington Consensus. He sees the Atlantic Alliance as the cornerstone of British foreign policy vital in preserving Britain's position in Europe and the globe. There is no radical streak in his political make-up. He may be a manipulator of public opinion but will not capitulate to the popular mood if it does not accord with his views. Religion may help to provide the burning eyes and fake humility that serve him well in speeches, but Mammon is a worldly god. Blair is a natural pander, and will always make up to those richer and more powerful than he. Politically, that means Washington.

The key to Blair's foreign policy is very simple. It was revealed in words of one syllable to Christopher Meyer, Blair's new Ambassador to Washington in 1997, by Jonathan Powell, the Prime Minister's Chief of Staff. On his appointment, Meyer explained to Blair's biographer, Powell gave him the following advice: 'Your job is to get up the arse of the White House and stay there.'[2] Maintaining this cosy, even intimate position has been the lodestar of Blair's strategy ever since. 'Whither thou goest, I will go', he is famous for having vowed to Clinton during an after dinner speech at the height of the Lewinsky affair. But as he packed his bags, Clinton made clear to Blair that this was not just personal. It was the British Premier's duty to forge an equally close relationship with the 44th President, whoever it might be.

---

[2] Anthony Seldon, *Blair*, London 2004, p. 370. This is by far the most useful and best-researched biography of the New Labour leader.

Blair had some rocky moments initially, as the Bush Administration made clear that it had little interest in this middle-ranking Atlantic state. Britain was anyway convulsed by petrol protests and foot and mouth disease. But as the B52s stuffed with daisy cutter bombs revved up for Operation Enduring Freedom, Blair went into hyperdrive. The war on terror was his war. He would see it through to its apocalyptic end. A secret Downing Street memorandum from 23 July 2002, leaked to the *Sunday Times* in May this year, reveals more about Blair's real thinking on Iraq than anything his speech-writers have been able to confect.[3] It confirms that, by July 2002, Bush had decided to go to war and had confided in Blair. Both these rogues were now devising plans to do so effectively.

> C reported on his recent talks in Washington. There was a perceptible shift in attitude. Military action was now seen as inevitable. Bush wanted to remove Saddam, through military action, justified by the conjunction of terrorism and WMD. But the intelligence and facts were being fixed around the policy.

Blair's main concern was how to fix the situation so the White House could get what it wanted. His government would 'work on the assumption that the UK would take part in any military action'. But the key issue was to have 'the political strategy to give the military plan the space to work'. To that end, a shallow plan was laid to

---

[3] *Sunday Times*, 1 May 2005. For the whole text of the memorandum, see Appendix One below.

trap Saddam into defying the UN (one which Saddam easily side-stepped, of course). Foreign Secretary Jack Straw busied himself to that end:

> The Foreign Secretary said he would discuss this with Colin Powell this week. It seemed clear that Bush had made up his mind to take military action, even if the timing was not yet decided. But the case was thin. Saddam was not threatening his neighbours, and his WMD capability was less than that of Libya, North Korea or Iran. We should work up a plan for an ultimatum to Saddam to allow back in the UN weapons inspectors. This would also help with the legal justification for the use of force.

It's clear that God had little part to play in these calculations. Far more central was to remain embedded in the President's nether regions. This was the level of strategic thinking that lay behind the invasion of Iraq and the bloody military occupation that has followed—and which has now blown back in the tragic events of July 7th.

Worse, this disastrous foreign policy has been pursued against the background of a hollowed-out national political life, and the solidification of a government–media consensus into an impenetrable bubble that precludes serious public debate about the country's direction. Eight years after the landslide that first swept New Labour into office, Margaret Thatcher's neoconservative project is more firmly in place than ever. A 'model' neo-liberal economy—the primacy of consumption, speculation as the hub of economic activity, the entry of private capital into hitherto inviolate domains of collective provision—reigns supreme.

An unrepresentative, unreformed electoral system; a foreign policy whose loyalty to Washington is comparable, in the novelist John Lanchester's memorable phrase, 'only to the coital lock which makes it impossible to separate dogs during sex'; the right to a jury trial and the presumption of innocence under heavy attack; an authoritarian social agenda; a conformist media, shamelessly used as a propaganda pillar for the new order—these are the principal characteristics of the British scene today. To these can be added the broader homogenization of national culture, with BBC managers desperately aping their commercial rivals; the virtual death of an indigenous cinema;[4] a relentlessly middlebrow theatre, where the boundaries between the boulevard and the subsidized theatres are rarely visible; the market-realist transformation of British publishing by global conglomerates; the ghettoisation of all thought that does not produce quick profits and the takeover of the universities by assessment-driven management dogma, in which academics are encouraged to refer to the student readers of their books as 'customers'. Political life in Britain has increasingly come to resemble that of a banana monarchy.

The transformation of the Labour Party has been part and parcel of this. Thatcher's electoral successes

---

[4] Ken Loach, Mike Leigh and a handful of others remain the exception, though in Loach's case the bulk of the funding comes from continental Europe.

during the 1980s had first traumatized and then hypnotized her supposed Labour opponents. She had transformed the Conservative Party, marginalizing its patricians and pushing it in a Poujadist direction from which it has not yet recovered. Tired of being defeated by Thatcher, Labour's leadership decided to mimic her success. In Blair they found the perfect cross-dresser.

Awestruck by Thatcher, the Blairites aped her achievements within their own party. The party conference, once a reflection of a vigorous inner-party debate that permitted ordinary members a voice, was totally recast. Presentation drowned what little politics still prevailed inside the party and journalists were reduced to recording the exact time of standing ovations. The trade-unions, promised a few stale crumbs, went along with the great transformation.

Thatcher's abrasiveness had alienated the liberal intelligentsia; astonishing to recall now, but in those days a majority of Oxford dons had deemed themselves independent enough to vote against giving the Prime Minister an honorary degree. The Blairites had no desire to reverse any of Thatcher's measures, but they saw her style as too harsh, too divisive. One had only to think of Norman Tebbit.[5] They would maintain the

---

[5] New Labour would produce its own Tebbit in the shape of David Blunkett. Obsessed with pleasing the *Daily Mail* and *Sun* readers, he soon became narcissistic about his own tough-man image. He would show criminals and asylum seekers who was master. The tabloids built him up as the strongman of the junta. It was only when he started whingeing after

Thatcher model but in a nicer, more touchy-feely way. Presentation and spin became a central feature.

Labour's metamorphosis into a party whose programme was virtually indistinguishable from the Conservatives (and in some respects—wars, arts, tuition fees—worse than that of the Major government) did not provoke any rebellion within its ranks, once the left had been crushed in the early 1980s. The trade unions had been brought to heel and the Party itself was ready for any Faustian pact as long as Blair could get them into office. Some, no doubt, genuinely believed that the shift was merely cosmetic. Once in power, Labour would revert to its old Keynesian self. Others, including converts from the old left, were in more 'realistic' mode. Capitalism was the only game in town and the rules had to change accordingly. The same dogma that had once characterized their Trotskyism or other isms was now put in the service of capital; former Cabinet ministers Milburn and Byers spring immediately to mind, but they were not alone.[6]

---

being dumped by the hyper-active publisher of the *Spectator* that the same tabloids decided it was time to bring him down. The tears shed in the *Guardian* and elsewhere for this 'heroic' son of the working class—the chief janitor of Belmarsh—were sickening.

[6] There was some initial recoil. In the summer of 1997 I encountered a senior Cabinet minister, a genial old Labour frontbencher, in a bookshop on Museum Street in Central London. 'What's it like?' I inquired. In response he held his nose. 'That bad?' 'Worse', he said, 'worse than even people like you could imagine.'

Slowly, the Blairites helped their colleagues to squeeze the old ideas out of themselves, drop by drop, until they woke up to find that the blood coursing through their veins was no longer that of independent human beings but that of the living dead. They happily went along with everything that was done. Accepting donations from Bernie Ecclestone to the party coffers and, as a consequence, delaying the ban on tobacco advertising? Fine. Private Finance Initiatives in the public services? Fine. Selling off schools suffering from financial undernourishment? Fine. The same applied to the war on Yugoslavia and the invasions of Afghanistan and Iraq.

The Parliamentary Labour Party has, with few exceptions, swallowed every bitter and nauseous pill that Blair and Campbell forced down its collective throat. If government ministers felt angry and humiliated, a combination of timidity and prudence sealed their lips. They knew full well that the knacker's yard beckoned, yet virtually none resigned. Most would only leave when pushed. Afterwards the rage poured out, but it was too late to be of any use.

Presiding over this constellation was the Dorian Gray-like figure of Tony Blair; the heavy make-up can no longer conceal the cracks and fissures. 'New, new, new, everything new', the Boy Leader is reported to have said, soon after taking office. It's true that, if Labour's socio-economic agenda has essentially been an unpleasant amalgam of Thatcher and Clinton, there has been something genuinely new in the degree of control over governmental processes that would soon be exercised by the propaganda and policy departments at Number Ten. With the exception of the Treasury, Blair's grip on state, media, church and party is unprecedented in modern times.

Thatcher's Cabinet had included some heavyweights, who ultimately brought her down. From the beginning, Blair's Cabinet—with the exception of Gordon Brown, who clung on desperately to his pound of flesh—was a weak and enfeebled outfit. It became even more so once Cabinet ministers or their civil servants had to clear everything with Alastair Campbell or Jonathan Powell.

Thatcher had always had a substantial section of the media and the intelligentsia against her. She was anathema not just to the Oxford dons mentioned above but to most of the country's writers, academics and programme-makers at Channel 4 and BBC 2. Though she had the backing of the Murdoch and Rothermere empires, the *Guardian*, *Mirror*, *Observer* and *Independent* were always against her. Blair, by contrast, has enjoyed virtually unanimous support from the *Sun* and *Economist* leftward. In the 2001 election he had the backing of the whole Murdoch stable—*The Times*, *Sunday Times*, *Sun*, *News of the World*—as well as the *Economist*, *Financial Times*, *Independent*, *Guardian*, *Express* and *Mirror*. The *Daily Mail* stayed silent. Only the *Telegraph* called for a Tory vote. As we shall see, this consensus has only hardened as the Blair government has lurched from one war to the next. Marching in step with Blair, the bulk of the liberal press is now either defending or covering up a murderous military occupation of Iraq, the widespread use of torture and a shoot-to-kill policy on London's streets.

'Christianity is a very tough religion', wrote Blair in 1993. 'It is judgemental. There is right and wrong. There is good and bad. We all know this, of course, but it has become fashionable to be uncomfortable about such language.'[7] Under his aegis, it's fashionable to be entirely comfortable about it. Religion does not explain Blair's warmongering; that is policy-driven. But it has helped to characterize its tone. New Labour's message has been very simple. We have no politics, we don't believe in social democracy but, despite the emptiness of our souls, there is a God. Blair is undoubtedly the most religious Prime Minister that Britain has thrown up since Gladstone. Not only does the deity exist, but a muscular Christianity is needed to fight on His behalf. A Republican in the United States, a Christian Democrat in Europe; on this side of the Channel the divine being is definitely New Labour.

Blair's inner circle is deeply tinged with the New Christianity. Thrusting young careerists, dreaming of a safe parliamentary seat when the old codgers die off, soon began to discover the deep spiritual gap in their lives which could only be filled with some form of Christianity.[8] Others are genuine believers, like the

---

[7] Quoted in John Kampfner, *Blair's Wars*, London 2003.

[8] Anyone who wants to understand why the Tories in Scotland have become virtually extinct should pay a visit to the Scottish Parliament and observe the New Labour species in action. A fair sprinkling of these young things, careerist to the core, regard Gordon Brown as too radical.

12

current Secretary of State for Education Ruth Kelly, a fervent supporter of Opus Dei. Blair's advisors have kept a wary eye on the packaging of his faith. When, in the run-up to the Iraq War, Blair wanted to conclude a TV address to the nation with the words, 'God bless you', there was a revolt from the assembled aides— Powell, Campbell, Mandelson, Hunter, etc. He ended his speech with a limp, 'Thank you'.

Whatever else, the Bible, Koran and Torah contain lyrical passages. These have had no impact on Blair. Could it really be the case, as a former intimate of his once confided to me, that, like Mrs Victoria Beckham, Blair has never read a whole book? The impoverishment of thought and language that characterizes our political culture can't be totally dissociated from the priorities of Number Ten. Blair, unlike Thatcher, Heath or Wilson, typifies the loss of a political vocabulary. In its place there is a great deal of vacuous moralism and, of course, religion. Blair has some thespian talents, and can perform in a range of different registers, from the blokeish 'I'm just an ordinary guy' to the Army chaplain, speeding the troops to their death, to his trademark, 'I honestly believe'. Hard truth, always difficult for politicians, has been replaced with the facile simulacrum of sincerity.

2

The Grammar of Deceit

The crisis of representation induced by the blanket consensus of the major parties and their respective media backers can lead to unexpected political explosions—the rough music unwelcome to those who inhabit the bubble. The rejection by French and Dutch voters of a draft EU Constitution that enshrined rule from above along free market lines was one such example; a rejection that would doubtless have been repeated in Britain had the government not cancelled the vote.

Across the advanced capitalist world the neo-liberal model has atomized social and political life, weakened democratic accountability and drastically reduced the margins of reformist possibilities within the system. Deindustrialization has led to the decline of organized labour and working-class parties. A giant advertising–entertainment complex moulds mass culture to the needs of the market. In Britain, this enfeeblement and hollowing out of the democratic process has proceeded even further than in much of continental Europe, thanks to the grotesque nature of its constitutional arrangements—its unrepresentative first-past-the-post electoral system, TV monarchy and unelected second chamber.

The British electoral system has helped to conceal the relentless ebbing of popular support for New Labour.

In 1997, some 13.5 million voted Labour (already fewer than the 14 million who had cast their ballots for John Major in 1992). In 2001, the Labour vote was down to 10.7 million. In 2005, it sank still further to 9.5 million—barely a fifth (a mere 21.8 per cent) of the overall electorate, the lowest level of support for a government in the EU, and comparing badly to the 32 per cent of Americans who voted for Bush.

Thanks to the prestidigitation of the winner-takes-all electoral system, however, these falling votes have continued to deliver overwhelming parliamentary majorities for Labour. In 2001, with turnout down to a record-breaking 59 per cent, Labour was allocated 413 seats, the Conservatives 166 and the Liberal Democrats 52 seats. In 2005, with turnout little better, the system awarded Labour 356 seats for 35 per cent of the vote; the Tories 198 seats for 30 per cent of the vote; and the Liberal Democrats a mere 62 seats for 22 per cent of the vote.

Nearly three million Labour voters in the old industrial heartlands of Northern England and the West Midlands decided to abstain. The entry of Starbucks into the old city centres had, alas, failed to override the deep sense of alienation and despair. The other major category of abstainers were the under-25s. 'We are a young country', some speech writer had inserted in one of Blair's election monologues. A majority of those between the ages of 18 and 25 did not vote in either 2001 or 2005. Gordon Brown, not known until then for an attachment to surrealism, provided an explanation: the reason so many people didn't vote is because they were happy with government policies. These abstentions, coupled with a massive decline of the Conservative vote (from 14 million in 1992 to 9.6 million in 1997, 8.3 million in 2001, 8.7 million in 2005), highlight the crisis of representation in the current system. Democratism has triumphed over democracy. The model towards which Britain is sliding is, of course, that of the United States. The poor don't bother to vote and the rich fork out $200 million or thereabouts to help their favoured candidate. Money rules and more money rules absolutely.

Blair had long remained insulated from the diminishing popularity of his policies, both by the parliamentary system and by the media bubble. Increasingly though, Blair has alienated a substantial section of the population. Inside the bubble, many were incredulous. 'A foreign policy issue helping to decide the election? Preposterous.' But it was true. The grammar of deceit employed by Blair and his ministers to support Washington's drive to war in the Middle East had alienated millions. These were by no means confined to traditional Labour voters, but extended to 'middle England'. More than once I heard people of moderate sensibilities use words to the effect that 'I used to approve of his politics, I admired his eloquence, ignored his reverence for the Church, but then came Iraq. He lied. I will never forgive him for the deception.'

Nor was the anger confined to ordinary citizens. Fifty former British ambassadors to the Arab world went public in their opposition to the war and in July 2003 Sir Rodric Braithwaite, former head of the Joint Intelligence Committee, wrote a remarkably prescient

letter to the *Financial Times* on the Labour government's
handling of the invasion of Iraq and the war on terror:

> If the current row rumbles on, demands for a judicial
> inquiry into the government's handling of intelligence
> on Iraq will doubtless grow. Meanwhile, there is little
> point in speculating on what an inquiry might turn up or
> its likely effects on the prime minister's fortunes.
>
> But the campaign to win round a sceptical public was
> not conducted primarily on the basis of intelligence dos-
> siers. In the first months of this year we were bombarded
> with warnings that British cities might at any moment
> face a massive terrorist attack. Housewives were offi-
> cially advised to lay in stocks of food and water. Tanks
> were sent to Heathrow airport. People were unwilling to
> go to war to uphold the authority of the United Nations,
> to overthrow an evil dictator in a distant country, or pro-
> mote democracy throughout the Middle East. But in this
> atmosphere of near hysteria, they began to believe that
> Britain itself was under imminent threat and that we
> should get our blow in first. And so the prime minister
> managed—just—to swing parliament behind him.
>
> What has happened since then? No weapons of mass
> destruction have been found. If they exist, they were so
> deeply hidden as to constitute no imminent threat to
> Britain. Official warnings of terrorist attacks on our
> cities have died away, though the incentives for terrorists
> to attack us have probably been increased, not dimin-
> ished, by the outcome of the war. Democracy seems as
> far off as ever from the troubled streets of Baghdad. All
> may yet be well. At present it does not much look like it.
>
> Fishmongers sell fish; warmongers sell war. Both
> may sincerely believe in their product. The prime min-
> ister surely acted in the best of faith. But it does look as
> though he seriously oversold his wares. The final judge-
> ment will be delivered not by the mandarins, the judges

or the politicians. It will be delivered by the consumer—the British public.[9]

The reason for the growing public anger with the government had little to do with any ideology. It was based on a strong instinct. People felt they were being fed untruths. In this respect, the response of the liberal press in Britain lagged far behind that in the United States. Mark Danner, writing in the *New York Review of Books*, suggested that the Cheney–Bush outfit was using its power to reshape the truth:

> Power, the argument runs, can shape truth: power, in the end, can determine reality, or at least the reality that most people accept—a critical point, for the administration has been singularly effective in its recognition that what is most politically important is not what readers of the *New York Times* believe but what most Americans are willing to believe. The last century's most innovative authority on power and truth, Joseph Goebbels, made the same point but rather more directly: 'There was no point in seeking to convert the intellectuals. For intellectuals would never be converted and would anyway always yield to the stronger, and this will always be "the man in the street". Arguments must therefore be crude, clear and forcible, and appeal to emotions and instincts, not the intellect. Truth was unimportant and entirely subordinate to tactics and psychology.'[10]

---

[9] *Financial Times*, 10 July 2003.

[10] Mark Danner, 'The Secret Way to War', *New York Review of Books*, 9 June 2005. Danner is the author of *Torture and Truth: America, Abu Ghraib, and the War on Terror*, New York 2004. Though the foreign policies pursued have been identical, liberals have found it much harder to criticize Blair's.

Sir Rodric Braithwaite's view, alas, did not find a mainstream political voice in the 2005 British general election. During the campaign itself many New Labour MPs, trying to make sure they were returned, avoided using Blair's photograph in their election addresses. Liberal pro-Blair columnists, fearful of defeat, coined a new slogan: 'Vote Blair, Get Brown'. But the Iraq War would not go away. The savage chaos created by the war and the occupation was visible each day on the internet, even though the extent of it was regularly underplayed by the bulk of the print media as well as the BBC and commercial broadcasters.

The 2005 election campaign was one of the most dismal in British history. On all the issues that mattered, the Conservatives supported their opponent—Tory leaders being awestruck by Blair just as he had once been by Thatcher. The Liberal Democrats did not make Iraq the central issue in the campaign, even though they had initially opposed the war and favoured withdrawing all British troops by December 2005. They were cursed with a weak leader incapable of even looking in the direction of the New Labour jugular. The Green Party and the recently formed Respect alliance did focus their campaign on Iraq, as did some individual Lib-Dem candidates and Military Families Against the War. Of these groups, Respect alone triumphed. George Galloway, expelled from the parliamentary party because of his strong stand on Iraq, now won a safe Labour seat in the East End of London.[11]

---

[11] Oona King, the local Labour MP, was a staunch supporter of the war and a Blair loyalist. Much was made of the

Elsewhere tribalism prevailed. Many anti-war activists failed to understand that New Labour 'represented a historic break' and that if the warmonger MPs were to be defeated it would need large-scale tactical voting throughout the country. This was the position I argued in public, shocking the tribalists:

> Meanwhile, as some (non-Labour) MPs contemplate impeaching Blair for lying and other misdemeanours, a general election draws near in Britain. What are we going to do? If Blair wins this election (as appears likely), he will claim, like Bush, that the country supports him in these difficult times. It is for this reason that those who opposed the war must think carefully before they cast their votes. Abstention is not a serious option. The aim should be to return an anti-war majority to the House of Commons. This requires tactical/intelligent voting in every constituency.
>
> Normally, people vote to assert their political sympathies. But this is not a normal general election. It will be the first opportunity to punish the warmongers and,

---

fact by New Labour loyalists and Jeremy Paxman of the BBC, that she was both non-white and Jewish, though what this had to do with her politics escapes me. During the Second World War the constituency had a large working class Jewish population which had elected the Communist Phil Piratin against Labour in 1945 and 1951. The Bengali Muslims, the latest migrants to the area, now chose to elect a white, male, non-Muslim because like him, they were extremely hostile to the war. They did so despite heavy pressure from Labour bigwigs and the anti-war Mayor of London, Ken Livingstone. Though no commentator has remarked on this it remains a fact that the Respect campaign in Bethnal Green offered a voice to young and old Muslims. The attraction in this area to groups advocating terror will, as a result, be much reduced.

given the undemocratic voting system, the votes cast for the Greens, Respect and others will have no impact, with a possible exception in Bethnal Green and Bow, east London, where George Galloway confronts the warmonger Oona King. It is possible that in some constituencies the Green/Respect vote could ensure the return of a warmonger, as we have seen in the odd byelection. So why not treat this election as special and take the politics of the broad anti-war front to the electoral arena? If the result is a hung parliament or a tiny Blair majority, it will be seen as a victory for our side. . . .

Despite the fact that politics has evaporated inside New Labour, the demonstration had its impact. A total of 139 Labour MPs voted against the war. Robin Cook resigned from the cabinet. Clare Short was pushed out. George Galloway, the most consistent opponent in parliament, was expelled from the Labour party. The Liberal Democrats, Scottish Nationalists and Plaid Cymru voted against as well. In constituencies where there are MPs belonging to the anti-war faction, one should vote for them despite disagreements on many other issues. In the warmonger constituencies we should vote tactically. In my north London constituency, the MP is Barbara Roche: pro-war and pro everything else this wretched government has done. I don't simply want to vote against her. I want her to be defeated. That is why I will vote Liberal Democrat. [12]

Blair won, but with a rock-bottom popular vote and a reduced parliamentary majority. A poignant moment on election night was when one of the Prime Minister's rival candidates, Reginald Keys, who had lost a son in Iraq, denounced the war and Blair's inhumanity, while

---

[12] 'Lib-Dem for a Day', *Guardian*, 26 March 2005.

a pale-faced victor looked on, compelled to stay still and take the rough music. It was then that I thought of him as Dorian Gray. What a contrast there was between the 'new, new, new, everything new' face we were shown in 1997, surrounded by Mandelson's Union Jacks, and the war-ravaged features of this much-despised politician in 2005. A number of British military families were consulting lawyers to see if Blair and Straw could be prosecuted according to international law. The war had gone badly wrong. The country was awash with propaganda, but the bloody images refused to go away.

3

The Media Cycle

During the long run-up to the invasion of Iraq, the British media were unequally divided. Rupert Murdoch, Lord Rothermere, Richard Desmond and the Barclay twins were for the war: this meant that that *The Times, Sun, Sunday Times, News of the World, Daily Telegraph, Sunday Telegraph, Daily* and *Sunday Express,* the *London Standard, Daily Mail* and *Mail on Sunday* were for it too. Add the pro-war *Observer* and *Financial Times* and there is a combined 2003 circulation figure of over 12 million. The *Mirror, Guardian* and *Independent*—total circulation 2.6 million—though expressing themselves unconvinced by the case for war, swung behind the troops when the moment came.[13]

---

[13] When Blair presented the dodgy WMD dossier to parliament in September 2002, Polly Toynbee gushed in the *Guardian*: 'a bravura performance, spellbinding in its quiet solemnity, reasoning the arguments, one by one.' The paper's editorial some months later was even more adulatory. Coverage in the *Independent* remained critical of the war, but editorially it faltered just before the war began: 'Blair has shown himself in the past few days to be at once the most formidable politician in the country and the right national leader for these deeply uncertain times.' Similar things were said in the Italian press about Mussolini prior to the invasions of Abyssinia and Albania. In his case the opposition was in prison. In Britain there was no official opposition at all as far as military adventures were concerned.

In the country as a whole, a majority was against the war. The million and a half who came out on the streets in February 2003 to try and halt the drift to disaster represented the largest public demonstration in British history, dwarfing the anti-Vietnam War movement of the 60s and 70s as well as the Chartists of the preceding century.

If the print media were solidly behind the warmongering Labour government, how did the BBC react? The Corporation generally views politics through the parliamentary prism. Divisions in parliament are faithfully represented on the BBC. But what if the government and opposition are in agreement, and the smaller third party isolated in adopting the Franco-German position on the war? The obvious criterion then would be the temperature of the country. As the countdown to war began, the two senior figures heading the BBC were both regarded as New Labour placemen. Gavyn Davies, the Chairman of the Board of Governors, was close to Gordon Brown, and Director-General Greg Dyke was an enthusiastic supporter of the Prime Minister and had helped to fund New Labour in 1997. When Dyke was appointed there had been much unfavourable comment. He was regarded as a Blair crony. Without going back to John Birt, it would have been difficult to find two men more sympathetic to the general outlook of New Labour.

And yet Blair fell out with both of them. The price of truth had become prohibitive. That Alastair Campbell, Number Ten's CSD (Chief Spin Doctor—not a Civil Service appointment) was out of control was hardly a secret. Rory Bremner and the Johns Bird and Fortune had lampooned Blair's dependence on his CSD to great effect.[14] For the print media it was easier to express hostility to Campbell than his master. Campbell and his beleaguered boss grew agitated as they watched the BBC's coverage of the big demonstration on 15 February. An enraged Campbell rang Dyke to denounce the BBC for accepting that there were a million people out on the streets. It was pointed out to him that this was the official police estimate. The demonstrators claimed a million and a half.

This was followed by anger at the composition of BBC *Question Time* audiences which were over-whelmingly hostile to the war, reflecting British public opinion. In order to appease Downing Street the BBC searched hard to find pro-war people (a majority sup-plied by friendly Kurds and Ahmed Chalabi's group in London) to 'balance' the audience. It was not enough. The CSD and Blair felt that the arm-twisting was not working and a more serious intervention was required. Blair decided to send a letter of complaint (drafted by his Campbell) to the Director-General. On 19 March 2003, a Prime Minister hell-bent on war wrote to the Chairman and Director-General of the BBC:

> It seems to me that there has been a real breakdown of the separation of news and comment . . . I believe and I am not alone in believing, that you have not got the balance

---

[14] In the often brilliant *Bremner, Bird and Fortune* programme on Channel 4.

right between support and dissent; between news and comment; between the voices of the Iraqi regime and the voices of Iraqi dissidents; or between the diplomatic support we have, and diplomatic opposition.

It was the CSD's bullying, intimidation and harassment of the BBC that provoked Dyke's robust response two days later:

Dear Tony

Thank you for your letter of 19 March. I note that a similar letter was sent to Gavyn Davies, the chairman of the BBC, and a longer version was sent to our director of news, Richard Sambrook. They will also be replying.

Firstly, and I do not mean to be rude, but having faced the biggest ever public demonstration in this country and the biggest ever backbench rebellion against a sitting government by its own supporters, would you not agree that your communications advisers are not best placed to advise whether or not the BBC has got its balance right between support and dissent?

Given these circumstances they are hardly in a position to make a reasoned judgement about the BBC's impartiality. You have been engaged in a difficult battle fighting for your particular view of the world to be accepted and quite understandably, you want that to be reported.

We, however have a different role in society. Our role in these circumstances is to try to give a balanced picture. It is perfectly legitimate for you or your advisers to complain about particular stories—journalism is an imperfect profession—and if we make mistakes, as we inevitably do, under my leadership we will always say we were wrong and apologise.

However, for you to question the whole of the BBC's output across a wide range of radio, television and online services because you are concerned about particular stories which don't favour your view is unfair.

I believe we have made major efforts to ensure that the issues and events surrounding Iraq have been properly reported. Let me explain how we have done that.

Some weeks ago I set up a committee which ...decided to prevent any senior editorial figures at the BBC from going on the anti-war march; it was that committee which insisted that we had to find a balanced audience for programmes like Question Time at a time when it was very hard to find supporters of the war willing to come on.

And it was that same committee when faced with a massive bias against the war among phone-in callers, decided to increase the number of phone lines so that pro-war listeners had a better chance of getting through and getting onto the programmes. All this was done in an attempt to ensure our coverage was balanced. That same committee has discussed on a number of occasions whether our reports from Baghdad needed to be qualified.

Until yesterday we have been of the opinion that our journalism has not been restricted in a way which required qualification as a matter of course and even yesterday, after the war started, our reporters did not have Iraqi 'minders' and were free to move around the city. At no point has their copy been checked before broadcast.

My point is that we have discussed these sorts of issues at length and made the best judgements we could. That our conclusions didn't always please Alastair is unfortunate but not our primary concern . . .

On many occasions in my time as director general, the Downing Street press office under Mr Campbell denied stories that later turned out to be true. I can list half a dozen. There was never a certainty that a denial from the government director of information meant the story wasn't true. It often meant the Downing Street press office simply didn't want it reported.

I can only assure you that under my leadership I will do everything in my power to defend the BBC's fairness, independence and impartiality.

My committee is now meeting on a daily basis and we discuss the reporting of the Iraq issue every morning . . .

I appreciate the fact that your letter was private. I, too, have no intention of making this reply public.

Best wishes

Greg Dyke

It is difficult to predict how the dispute would have ended had not Dr David Kelly— a government scientist specializing in chemical weapons— been found dead close to his home in the English countryside on 18 July 2003. Kelly had in separate off-the-record discussions with two BBC journalists cast doubt on the government's case for war. One of these journalists, Andrew Gilligan, using Kelly as an unnamed source, went public on Radio 4's *Today* programme and said that government had used 'sexed up' evidence to justify the war. As is well known now this was indeed the case. A government committed to sticking with Washington's war drive at any price was inventing pretexts for its policy. Gilligan stumbled onto this and, precisely because it was true, he struck several raw nerves in the Downing Street propaganda machine. Tabloid clichés emanating from briefings at Number Ten indicated that Campbell had 'gone ballistic', would 'skewer the BBC', etc. One thing was clear. The CSD had become obsessed with the BBC and wanted heads to roll. Someone had to be punished. At that stage Downing Street would have been happy if Gilligan had been sacrificed. Accordingly, the government publicly demanded an apology from the Corporation. To its enormous credit, the BBC refused. War was declared.

Blair and his CSD then decided to out Kelly as the BBC source, which resulted in the scientist being forced to attend a bruising session of the Commons Select Committee on Foreign Affairs. It was the mauling he received here that led to his apparent suicide. Kelly's death, combined with the fierce and growing resistance in Iraq throughout the summer of 2003, created a crisis for the Labour government. Blair, en route to Tokyo and for once without his CSD, was struck dumb by the news. It was obvious that decisions taken at Downing Street had led to Kelly's death, but the blame was transferred straight to the BBC. How would all this end?

Enter stage right, in time-honoured fashion, the good Lord Hutton, a tried and tested servant of the state, to preside on his own over an official inquiry into the circumstances that led to the death of Dr Kelly. In his memoirs, Greg Dyke quotes Philip Gould, a debased member of Blair's inner sanctum, reassuring a worried Labour peer: 'Don't worry, we appointed the right judge.' An email confirming Gould's judgement from an old friend of mine in Northern Ireland greeted me on the computer in the form of a football chant: 'He's safe, he's sound, he's a Diplock hound!'[15] The then Sir Brian Hutton had firsthand experience of being supportive to a government after political disaster. In 1972 he had represented the British Army at the infamous Widgery Inquiry into the events of Bloody Sunday, now acknowledged as a total whitewash.

This was not the view of the Secretary of State for Constitutional Affairs Lord Falconer, who described Hutton as an 'unimpeachable judge' who will 'not produce a whitewash.'[16] The evidence published online every day during the first phase of the inquiry in the summer of 2003 allowed an extraordinary insight into the corrupt political culture of Number Ten. Many thought that Blair would not survive. Even a Diplock Judge would be shaken by the weight of the evidence. But such is not the British system. During his testimony, Blair was well protected by his appointee against

---

[15] The Diplock courts were established (in response to a report by Lord Diplock) by the British government in Northern Ireland in 1972, in an attempt to deal with Loyalist and IRA violence in the province. The right to trial by jury was suspended and the court consisted of a single judge. The courts were meant to be an alternative to the internment without trial, also in force at the time, and became a byword for state corruption. The judges appointed to these courts, which have yet to be fully 'phased out', were carefully vetted for their reliability. Lord Hutton was one of them. Hence the total lack of surprise in Northern Ireland when the Hutton Report was published.

[16] And a few journalists. 'Public inquiries over the years have slapped on the whitewash,' Nick Cohen wrote in the pro-war *Observer*, 17 August 2004, only to insist: 'This time it's completely different'.

any serious cross-examination by the BBC lawyers. Hutton's tone was deferential, in sharp contrast to the treatment of Greg Dyke.[17] The report, when it finally appeared on 28 January 2004 was, as widely expected, a whitewash.

That was not enough for the CSD. Campbell immediately called a press conference in the lush headquarters of the Foreign Press Association where, like a 'rooster on a dungheap',[18] he crowed how he had been completely vindicated and hinted at vengeance. Campbell's schoolboyish flamboyancy, devious mind and overpitched ambitions had this time gone too far. This performance is said to have lost him his job. Vaudeville beckoned.

The death of David Kelly, the Hutton apologia and the Downing Street antics that followed aroused a great

---

[17] The libertarian essayist James Heartfield summed up the contradictions well: 'Andrew Gilligan's original report, it should be said, was a useful piece of journalism. He had evidence that the report had been 'sexed up' at the instigation of the Prime Minister's press secretary Alastair Campbell, and that it caused disquiet in the intelligence community. But Hutton managed to side-step those issues by alighting on Gilligan's allegation that the government introduced the claim that Iraqi leader Saddam Hussein had WMD warheads set for use in 45 minutes, knowing it to be probably false. It was this charge that the government had lied that Blair and Campbell fixed on, and that Hutton showed could not be substantiated . . . In the topsy-turvy world of Lord Hutton's enquiry, then, it could be proved that the Prime Minister was not lying when he said that there were Weapons of Mass Destruction—just as key figures in the US administration were acknowledging that there never had been any.'

[18] The description popularized by Max Hastings.

deal of anger throughout the country, and especially 'middle England' which valued the BBC highly. The mood was eloquently expressed in Alan Bennett's contribution to the *London Review of Books:*

2 February 2004. There is nothing that has not been said. Some notes, though. Revealing, since his vanity was the main issue, were the settings in which Alastair Campbell chose to present himself: two Palladian interiors that would not have shamed a head of state. His simple joy at the vindication of the truth about as convincing as Jonathan Aitken's dedication to it.

Almost the only heartening note was the outright condemnation of the BBC's apology (and its abjectness) by its most distinguished broadcaster, David Attenborough. With a constituency that far outnumbers that of the Labour Party and a voice that is more respected and indeed loved than any politician's can hope to be, if David Attenborough is on the other side, the government ought to be worried. It also ought to be ashamed, of course, but we're long past that.

What happens when the BBC's charter comes up for renewal is anybody's guess. I would place no reliance on the word of the fragrant Tessa Jowell, who keeps rattling the charter, then pretending she hasn't. She needs to be watched: she may be a weasel in talcum powder.

One person who saw it coming was Ludovic Kennedy who, hearing Hutton named to head the inquiry, correctly predicted the outcome. I looked up the judge, then Sir Brian Hutton, in Kennedy's *Thirty-Six Murders,* where he pinpoints one of Hutton's shortcomings back in 1995 as a failure to notice non sequiturs. There was going to be a lot more of that.

Hutton has a look of the actor Bernard Archard, who specialised in policemen of the middle rank who played things by the book. Saying what he feels is required, Lord Hutton would have done well as counsellor to Henry VIII. Trim and somehow spry he has the same tap-dancing figure as an earlier servant of the law, Lord Diplock.

It cannot be stated too often that Blair decided on war, then looked round for its justification and thinking he had found it bumped the country along with him. Robin Cook is careful always to give Blair the benefit of the doubt, saying that Blair really did believe Saddam had the weapons. I'm never sure, though, that Cook's forbearance is not just an extension of the parliamentary convention that you don't accuse a fellow member of lying. If Blair knew that the weapons he was talking about were tactical battlefield weapons but which, their nature unspecified, he also knew would be thought by the public to be long-range devices, to leave this misapprehension uncorrected, as Hoon admits that he did, invalidates Cook's assumption about the prime minister's honour. Not in Hutton, of course. Not his remit. And not, if Blair gets his way, in the remit of the next report either. And so we go on.

The person entitled to feel most immediately aggrieved by the report is Mrs Kelly. But I suspect that along with all his other received assumptions Lord Hutton regards suicide as a weakness and one that need not detain us long, the whole report almost a dictionary definition of what is meant by 'a safe pair of hands'.

Blair's promise to the BBC bosses that there would be no reprisals was soon proved hollow. The BBC Board of Directors were prepared to sacrifice Gavyn Davies but Dyke had been openly critical of the Hutton Report and Downing Street wanted his head as well. Both men were sacked. The true colours of Blair's banana monarchy were never more apparent. The temporary replacements at the Corporation bowed and scraped and apologized in public like disgraced bureaucrats in Honecker's Germany.

Helping Blair to reshape the BBC from behind the scenes was its former boss and Labour peer, John Birt. It was Birt's protégé, Mark Thompson, who replaced Dyke and, a few months into his watch, told the heads of Current Affairs that their perceptions of the government were regarded as being too negative. This was hardly news to BBC journalists, but the message was clear. The sad decline of BBC World and the news bulletins accelerated rapidly. Few traces now remain of serious investigative journalism, leave alone solid criticism.[19]

Inside the Corporation the New Labour clampdown had created a mood of anger and despair. As Dyke came to collect his belongings there were emotional displays of solidarity by working journalists, unprecedented in BBC history. They knew he had defended them against power. For an influential clique of toadies at the *Financial Times*, however, Number Ten's decision to sack the Director-General of the BBC—essentially, for having broadcast doubts about the existence of Iraq's WMD—was an opportunity to prove that subservience to the Blair government would come before every

---

[19] The Conservative government of John Howard in Australia followed the same path in neutering the Australian Broadcasting Corporation. The diversity fostered by Blair and Howard is well illustrated by the 247 editors in Murdoch's pay in different parts of the globe: each and every one of them supported the war in Iraq.

scruple. John Lloyd, the editor of the *FT* magazine, a weekly bugle call to march behind Blair and Bush, argued that Hutton had vindicated the sword of truth:

> Can journalism tell the truth? It has always been one of its proclaimed aims. There are many others that occupy more of the media's time, including entertainment, profit-making and creation of celebrities. But telling the truth should be journalism's gold standard. Is it possible to believe in journalistic truth after the BBC, a broadcasting service seen as one of the most objective in the world, was charged this week with distorting the facts? Did the broadcaster—condemned by the Hutton report—fail because it did not tell the truth? The answer to both these questions, for journalists everywhere, is yes . . . The BBC, which has led the world in the provision of explanatory TV, has retreated from it, to concentrate on the studio clash. It has increasingly gone for overturning stones, or sensational revelations, in this case the framework within which the reporter Andrew Gilligan made his now notorious charge that the government had knowingly lied in the creation of its Iraq dossier.[20]

Lloyd seems to have forgotten, despite his years in Moscow as an apologist for Boris Yeltsin, that the word for 'truth' in Russian is *pravda*. But he had the backing of his editor and political editor at the *Financial Times*. The latter, James Blitz, had already explained on 10 January 2004 that the main duty of the press in its relations with those in power was to find 'areas of consensus':

> Some will look to Lord Hutton's report to explain whether Britain was justified in going to war with Iraq. Others

---

[20] *Financial Times,* 29 January 2004.

will focus on whether there will be top-level resignations. But the central point of interest for me will be what light Lord Hutton throws on the civil war between the media and politicians. And whether the protagonists—the government, the BBC, the print media—make a serious effort to find areas of consensus.[21]

At the end of January 2004 Andrew Gowers, the *FT* editor, gave another lesson in good journalism. Here, the real sin was to 'demonstrate independence'. I quote at length to avoid accusations of 'sentences taken out of context' and to enable the reader to appreciate the joys of responsible and supportive journalism:

> What I am about to say may seem perverse, even shocking, at the end of a week like this one. But here goes: British journalists owe Andrew Gilligan a debt of gratitude.
>
> The BBC reporter whose misguided stories on the government's case for war in Iraq landed his employer in crisis exposed poor editing, deteriorating journalistic values and sloppy management at all levels of Britain's public service broadcaster.
>
> But he should also be remembered as the journalist who held up the mirror to British journalism as a whole, exposing its foibles and its faults. For while the crisis at the BBC is deep-seated, it is merely part of a broader malaise in British politics and media. And while radical reform of the corporation's management is undoubtedly necessary, the need for reassessment does not stop there . . .
>
> Now, all broadcasters and newspapers, including this one, make mistakes. Even the greatest can occasionally

---

[21] *Financial Times*, 10 January 2004.

run off the rails, as *The New York Times* did with its rogue reporter scandal last year.

But it is hard to imagine a graver charge against a media organisation than the one Lord Hutton levelled against the BBC. In reply, Mr Davies insinuates that Lord Hutton's conclusions do not fit the facts and mutters about threats to press freedom. And Mr Dyke claims the Gilligan story—though mistaken—was in the public interest and that the governors had no reason to apologise. In so doing, both demonstrate that they have only a passing acquaintance with the basic tenets of good journalism.

The flaws in Mr Gilligan's story should have been obvious from the moment he went on air. It was based on the testimony of one source, when most good editors—especially when it comes to contentious stories—insist on independent verification. It was vaguely phrased, unedited (at least in the notorious May 29 'two-way') and changed by Mr Gilligan from one broadcast or newspaper column to the next. The source, it subsequently emerged, was misdescribed—and could not have known in sufficiently complete detail about the matters on which he was being made to comment.

Against this background, Mr Dyke's contention that the thrust of the story was worth reporting, and that any mistakes were in the detail, defies belief. Worse, it demonstrates the extent to which the BBC has been infected by the poisonous culture that has long since tainted other parts of the discourse between politicians and the media. For Mr Dyke and Mr Davies, it was more important to resist and oppose the government than to check or correct an erroneous broadcast. In other words, an agenda, born of a desire to demonstrate independence, got in the way of the truth.[22]

---

[22] Andrew Gowers, 'The BBC's failings are a warning to all journalists', *Financial Times*, 31 January 2004.

Now one can understand why the *FT*'s coverage of Iraq has been so abysmal compared to even, say, that of the *New York Times*. It is, indeed, more comparable to *Pravda*'s.[23] One of the criticisms made is that Gilligan's story was based on only 'one source'. One could argue that often the stories published by responsible journalists of the Gowers/Lloyd school of journalism are based on one source: the CSD at 10 Downing Street. And how should even the most responsible toady read David Manning's July 2002 Downing Street memo?

A few weeks later Lloyd was attacking Dyke again, this time for his 'populism'—arguing that the former D-G 'saw success as constantly beating the competition, and in doing so was willing to sacrifice much in the way of current affairs and even broadcast news.'[24] But the BBC's accommodation to market-realism had begun under Sir John Birt, OBN, a Blair loyalist provided with a small berth at Downing Street, whose

---

[23] This recalls the tempest in a coffee cup provoked by Lloyd when, soon after 9/11, the *London Review of Books* rejected an article by David Marquand in which he referred to Blair's leadership as 'impeccable'. A small hue and cry was begun about 'censorship'. Censorship? The entire print media was full of praise for Blair's 'leadership qualities'. A literary magazine declined an article which said exactly the same and this was censorship. And this from John Lloyd who has yet to publish anything seriously critical of Blair or Bush in his own magazine. There are limits to toadyism. Ironically enough, David Marquand subsequently wrote sharp criticisms of Blair and refused to back the war machine.

[24] John Lloyd, 'Selling out to the market', *British Journalism Review*, 15 April 2004.

views on 'truth' and 'mission to explain' are, in fact, shared by Lloyd. Birt had taken Thatcher and Tebbit's attacks on the BBC as an indication that they were preparing to privatize it and, in response, had created an internal market structure and stifled creativity. Market norms were in place and the chaos that resulted and the management-speak that justified it was chronicled regularly in *Private Eye*.

Thatcher had sacked Alasdair Milne, hardly a turbulent Director-General, but too irresponsible for the times. Birt was the replacement who made the powerful happy: a man devoid of all instincts except the instinct to please. The process was continued after 1997, encouraged by a New Labour government which continually denounced 'elitist values' and pandered to tabloid populism. Nor should one underestimate the desire of both Thatcher and Blair to please Rupert Murdoch. The indulgence he has been shown is well documented.

Lloyd's criticism was therefore beside the point, given that Dyke had become an unlikely hero of free-thinking journalists throughout the country precisely because he stood up to Blair and defended the right to criticize a government in times of war. If, Mammon forbid, John Lloyd were to be sacked by his employers, how many of his journalist colleagues would stand on the pavements and weep? Possibly his fellow bugler Ian Buruma. Anyone else?

Even prior to Blair's election triumph in 1997, Peter Mandelson, his CSD at the time, had access to a group of liberal journalists who were happy to act as sieves.

After the victory their numbers grew. Martin Kettle of the *Guardian*, who used to boast that he often played tennis with the Dear Leader, was now happy to be a ballboy. Kettle's columns were the most predictable and he was demoted to leader writing, which explains why so many of the *Guardian* editorials are sycophantic pro-government drivel. The ballboy has recently informed his readers how he prefers Nicolas Sarkozy and Angela Merkel to their socialist opponents. Here, too, he is speaking in his master's voice. That such an open stooge of Number Ten should be the chief leader writer at the *Guardian* should be somewhat problematic.

At the *Observer* Andrew Rawnsley has remained a solid Blair/Mandelson loyalist, even given insider information to write the odd book in which the principal target was Gordon Brown. The debased David Aaronovitch (better suited to be a cheerleader for New Labour election agents than a journalist) was moved pawn-like from the *Independent* to the *Guardian* and has recently crossed over painlessly to *The Times*.

Pro-Blair, pro-war, pro-government, this is the new supportive journalism. Indeed, as his wars began, Blair acquired a new set of admirers, men and women who had earlier been extremely critical of the entire New Labour project, but were impressed by the 'humanitarian interventions' from 30,000 feet over Kosovo and Baghdad. These included Nick Cohen (*Observer*), Francis Wheen (*Private Eye*), Yasmin Alibhai-Brown and Johann Hari (*Independent*) and others.

Nor was this a purely British phenomenon. 'Putrefaction', Marx once wrote, 'is the laboratory of life', and a swarm of further examples can be found in France, Germany, Brazil and, of course, the United States. These journalists are, in the main, former liberal or leftists, including a few who were once staunch Marxists, but who have now accepted the 'superiority' of the West. Most are uncritical supporters of Israel. The vigilantism they propose in the Middle East must, of necessity, be selective. In one of his last essays, the late Edward Said described these capitulations with characteristic bluntness. It was, he argued, however masked, a belated conversion to the merits of colonialism.

> Revisionist justifications of the invasion of Iraq and the American war on terrorism that have become one of the least welcome imports from an earlier failed empire, Britain, and have coarsened discourse and distorted fact and history with alarming fluency, are proclaimed by expatriate British journalists in America who don't have the honesty to say straight out, yes, we are superior and reserve the right to teach the natives a lesson anywhere in the world where we perceive them to be nasty and backward. And why do we have that right? Because those woolly-haired natives whom we know from having ruled our empire for 500 years and now want America to follow, have failed: they fail to understand our superior civilisation, they are addicted to superstition and fanaticism, they are unregenerate tyrants who deserve punishment and we, by God, are the ones to do the job, in the name of progress and civilisation. [25]

---

[25] *Al-Ahram Weekly*, 21–27 August 2003.

43

4

The Days of July

British politicians have learnt from their American superiors that there is one continent to which they can always turn to burnish their do-gooding credentials in times of war or scandal. If Africa did not exist, rich-world governments would have to invent it. The need was great in July 2005. The war in Iraq was going badly, the EU Constitution débâcle had been an embarrassingly large-scale defeat for Blairite free-marketism on the continent, and the British economy was starting to splutter. As the leaders of the G8 gathered for their Summit in Scotland, hosted by Blair, Iraq was naturally banished from the public agenda and anti-war marchers were banned from the barricaded Gleneagles Hotel. The Summit was designed as a feel-good-do-nothing affair. Poverty in Africa—in large part the result of vicious IMF and World Bank restructuring programmes, as well as the debt burdens imposed by those institutions—would be magicked away, as if in a rerun of the miracle of loaves and fishes.

Blair's favourite courtier from the musical world, Bob Geldof, was hired to organize an extravaganza in Edinburgh that would hopefully attract the crowds away from anti-war protests. Geldof is a specialist in make-the-locals-feel-good events. He certainly makes the Prime Minister feel loved. A photograph of Blair and Geldof in the press showed a flirtatious musician resting his head on the Dear Leader's shoulder. I was pleased to see that the photo opportunities with Gordon Brown were more sober. Geldof, like the G8 leaders, is deeply concerned about poverty in Africa, and organizes a concert to prove it every twelve years. But the razzmatazz would soon be upstaged in London.

On 7 July 2005 a deadly quartet of three young Yorkshire Muslims and a Jamaican-born co-religionist from Aylesbury, their rucksacks loaded with explosives, blew themselves up more or less simultaneously, three of them at different points on the London Underground and one on a bus in Russell Square, not far from the British Museum. Fifty-six people died as a result and a hundred or so were wounded. Coming at the height of the rush-hour, the victims of this senseless carnage were mainly young office-workers; statistically, it's unlikely that more than one in five of them voted for Blair. It was a horrendous act, politically and morally unjustifiable. But there was no mystery as to why it had happened. Before the invasion, the Mayor of London, Ken Livingstone, had warned Blair of the consequences of dragging the country into an unpopular war: 'An assault on Iraq will inflame world opinion and jeopardize security and peace everywhere. London, as one of the major world cities, has a great deal to lose from war and a lot to gain from peace, international cooperation and global stability.'

This was not, of course, the first time that London and other British cities had been targeted by bombers opposing the British government. After 'Bloody

Sunday', the IRA brought the Irish war to mainland Britain for the last phase of 'the troubles'. They came close to blowing up Margaret Thatcher and her Cabinet when they bombed the Grand Hotel in Brighton during a Conservative Party conference. Later, IRA members fired a missile from a moving van at 10 Downing Street. London's financial quarter was also hit, causing immense damage to property. The successive Prevention of Terrorism Acts passed by the House of Commons, the introduction of 'internment without trial' and the general massacring of civil liberties both in Northern Ireland and on the mainland did nothing to prevent these and other attacks. There were lessons to be learnt from this history, as I argued in a short comment for the *Guardian* the day after the July 7th bombings:

> The majority of Londoners (as the rest of the country) were opposed to the war in Iraq. Tragically, it is they who have suffered the blow and paid the price for the re-election of Blair and a continuation of the war. Ever since 9/11, I have been arguing that the 'war against terror' is immoral and counterproductive. It sanctions the use of state terror—bombing raids, tortures, countless civilian deaths in Afghanistan and Iraq—against Islamo-anarchists whose numbers are small, but whose reach is deadly. The solution then, as now is political, not military. The British ruling elite understood this perfectly well in the case of Ireland. Security measures, anti-terror laws rushed through Parliament, identity cards, a general curtailment of civil liberties of British citizens will not solve the problem. If anything, they will push young Muslims in the direction of a mindless violence.
>
> The real solution lies in immediately ending the occupation of Iraq, Afghanistan and Palestine. Just because

these three wars are reported sporadically and mean little to the everyday life of most of Europe's citizens, this does not mean that the anger and bitterness they arouse in the Muslim world and its diasporas is insignificant. Establishment politicians have little purchase with the young and this applies especially strongly in the Arab world. As long as Western politicians wage their wars and their colleagues in the Muslim world watch in silence, young people will be attracted to the groups who carry out random acts of revenge. At the beginning of the G8, Tony Blair suggested that 'poverty was the cause of terrorism'. This is not so. The principal cause of this violence is the violence that is being inflicted on the people of the Muslim world. The bombing of innocent people is equally barbaric in Baghdad, Jenin, Kabul as it is in New York, Madrid or London. And unless this is recognized the horrors will continue.[26]

The following day I was denounced in the *Guardian* Letters column with an unsurprising degree of illiberal acrimony; what was more surprising was that not a single letter appeared in support of my position, since during the course of the next three days I received an exceptionally large email inbox, some 672 messages. Usually, after a public intervention I receive a maximum of a hundred or so missives and the supporters:critics ratio averages at 80:20. On this occasion it was 95:5. It was obvious that many people had immediately linked the bombings to the outrages committed by the Anglo-American occupiers of Afghanistan and Iraq, and that they did not like the way debate on the subject was being sidelined.

---

[26] 'The Price of Occupation', *Guardian*, 8 July 2005.

This linkage between the horrific London bombings and the horrors of the Middle East was exactly what the political-media bubble was determined to prevent. Here the propaganda machinery was in full flow. The regime and its apologists united in blocking out any mention of a connection with Iraq. It took the Liberal Democratic leader a whole week to mutter something to the effect that it was possible that there might be some link to the war in Iraq. He was immediately denounced by Downing Street for breaching the consensus agreed inside the bubble.

From Gleneagles, Blair's immediate response to the bombings had been predictably Bushite. Barbarians were attacking 'our civilization'. No other explanation would be countenanced. Why were these 'barbarians' not targeting Paris or Berlin? Why Madrid and London? Could it be that these appalling acts had something to do with the continuing war in Iraq where the 'civilized' conquerors do not even bother to count the Iraqi dead? That these questions were not confined to anti-war activists was confirmed by Alan Cowell, writing in the *New York Times* on 8 July 2005:

> Perhaps the crudest lesson to be drawn was that, in adopting the stance he took after the Sept. 11 attacks, Mr. Blair had finally reaped the bitter harvest of the war on terrorism—so often forecast but never quite seeming real until the explosions boomed across London. The war in Iraq has been increasingly unpopular here, with taunts that Mr. Blair had become President Bush's poodle. The anger about Iraq led to Mr. Blair's shaky showing in the May elections: a third term with a severely reduced majority.

Now, as long predicted and feared, his support of the war appears to have cost British lives at home. Thursday was a day of rallying behind the leader, but there were indications that the bombing could take a political toll.

The following week, an opinion poll—unusually, tucked away on an inside page of the newspaper that had commissioned it—revealed that 66 per cent of the population believed there was a link between Blair's decision to invade Iraq and the terror attacks in London.[27] Tame journalists and Labour ministers who had justified the war—Straw, Reid and the rest—still refused to accept there was any connection between the savage chaos in Baghdad and the bombs in London. On 26 July, Blair arrogantly reiterated his position:

> We are not having any of this nonsense about [the bombings having anything] to do with what the British are doing in Iraq or Afghanistan, or support for Israel, or support for America, or any of the rest of it. It is nonsense and we have to confront it as that.

Yet Foreign Office officials had warned the government in May 2004, over a year before the the bombs hit London, that the war in Iraq was stoking the fires of extremism in Muslim communities in Britain. In a letter addressed to the Cabinet Secretary, Sir Andrew Turnbull, the Permanent Under-Secretary at the Foreign Office Michael Jay had spelled it out for Downing Street:

> Other colleagues have flagged up some of the potential underlying causes of extremism that can affect the

---

[27] *Guardian*, 19 July 2005.

Muslim community, such as discrimination, disadvantage and exclusion. But another recurring theme is the issue of British foreign policy, especially in the context of the Middle East Peace Process and Iraq . . . Experience of both ministers and officials working in this area suggests that the issue of British foreign policy . . . plays a significant role in creating a feeling of anger and impotence amongst especially the younger generation of British Muslims . . . this seems to be a key driver behind recruitment by extremist organizations (e.g. recruitment drives by groups such as Hizb ut-Tehrir and al Muhajiroon).[28]

The political motives of suicide bombers have been underlined by Robert Pape, a US academic working on a University of Chicago project on suicide terrorism. Pape has analysed such attacks in very great detail and produced a serious and sober study of suicide terrorism over the past 25 years. It should be compulsory reading for members of the British government. Pape analyses 315 suicide terror attacks during this period and concludes that 'there is little connection between suicide terrorism and Islamic fundamentalism or any of the world's religions'. Instead:

what nearly all suicide terrorist attacks have in common is a specific secular and strategic goal: to compel modern democracies to withdraw military forces from the territory that the terrorists consider to be their homeland. Religion is rarely the root cause, although it is often used as

---

[28] Martin Bright, 'Leak shows Blair told of Iraq war terror link', *Observer*, 28 August 2005. The full text of the Jay letter is available on the Guardian Unlimited website.

a tool by terrorist organizations in recruiting and in other efforts in service of the broader strategic objective.[29]

This analysis is confirmed by the stories of the July 7th bombers, and of the pathetic group that apparently attempted further London Transport bombings on July 21st, but whose rucksacks failed to explode. Osman Hussain, suspected of trying to set off an explosion at Warren Street Station on July 21st, fled the country by Eurostar and was arrested in Italy a few weeks later. According to *La Repubblica*, he told investigators that the would-be bombers of July 21st had psyched themselves for the attacks by watching 'films on the war in Iraq . . . Especially those where women and children were being killed and exterminated by British and American soldiers . . . of widows, mothers and daughters that cry.'

The discrepancy between the price tag the Western media place on their own citizens—the photos of smiling faces, the intimate details recalled by friends and family—and on the tens of thousands of those nameless, uncounted bodies shot, tortured or blown up from 30,000 feet on the command of Bush and Blair, could hardly be starker. It is this that fuels the anger.

Further direct evidence of the political motives of the terrorists came in the ghoulish video tape left behind by Mohammed Siddique Khan, one of the July 7th suicide terrorists, and later broadcast by al-Jazeera TV. (His friends in Dewsbury, of whom there are many since he

---

[29] Robert Pape, *Dying to Win: The Strategic Logic of Suicide Terrorism*, New York 2005.

was a popular youth worker, claimed the tape was a fake. Perhaps deep down they did not want to believe that their friend had become a terrorist or maybe the denial was a way of protecting themselves from hostile journalists.) Speaking in a strong Yorkshire accent, Siddique Khan stated: 'Your democratically elected governments continuously perpetuate atrocities against my people and your support of them makes you directly responsible.' With Blair now off holidaying at Cliff Richard's luxury villa in Barbados, the British government response was left to Foreign Secretary Jack Straw, who still refused to accept this, insisting that British support for Bush had not made the country more vulnerable to terrorism.

To explain the cause is not to justify the consequence, but Blair and his toadies should be forced to confront what is now a widely held view across the political divide: the central British role in the occupations of Iraq and Afghanistan and, more broadly, Britain's unquestioning support for the US–Israeli war drive in the Middle East and across central Eurasia, has blown back in the shape of the London terrorist attacks. The reason the Prime Minister and his close associates in government and the media cannot admit the link is not difficult to understand. To accept that British foreign policy is even partially responsible means to accept that Blair, Straw and the rest of the supine Cabinet and the official Opposition are to blame for what is taking place. If Blair were to do so he would be immediately compelled to resign.

5

A Public Execution 'In Good Faith'

Jean Charles de Menezes (1978–2005)

Faced with this crisis, what has been the response of Blair's security forces? Though incapable of checking passports at the Waterloo Eurostar terminal, the state's armed thugs appear to have been given a virtual *carte blanche* to take things into their own hands. The result has been not only abysmal policing but human tragedy, as officers implemented the new 'shoot to kill' instructions recommended by Israeli security, without checking who their victim was.

The day after the failed bomb attacks of July 21st a special security unit was posted outside an address apparently found in one of the unexploded bags. This was a flat inside a three storey block in Tulse Hill in South London. The block contained nine apartments. One of these housed a 27 year-old Brazilian electrician and his two cousins.

Jean Charles de Menezes was born in a farm in Gonzaga, in the Brazilian state of Minas Gerais. His father was a bricklayer but wanted his children to be educated so they could have a better life. Jean Charles was a bright kid obsessed with electronics. In his teens his father encouraged him to leave the farm and move to São Paulo, where his uncle lived. It was here that he went to a state school and obtained a diploma. But employment opportunities were scarce in the city unless one was in hock to a politician's client network. Menezes applied for a work visa to the United States but was turned down. Desperate for work, he applied for a tourist visa to Britain in 2002. Once in London, he applied for and was given a student visa until 2003. He learnt English and began to work as an electrician. His cousins later revealed that his obsession was to start a cattle ranch back in Brazil and he was trying to earn as much money as he could as a freelance electrician so that he could return to Minas Gerais. It was not to be.

At 9.30 am on 22 July 2005, Jean Charles walked out of his flat to the bus stop from where he would board the Number 2 for the two-mile journey to Stockwell Underground Station. The surveillance team saw him and one of their number felt 'it would be worth some-one else having a look'. The 'someone else' was clearly 'Gold Command', the senior officer charged with giving clearance for the 'shoot-to-kill' policy back at Scotland Yard. But there was a problem. The surveillance officer with the video camera who thought Menezes might be the 'suspect' on their list was urinating at the time and could not, as a result, operate the camera to film Menezes and transmit the pictures to the Yard for further analysis. Who were these surveillance officers? One of the better informed accounts was provided by James Cusick, a Scottish journalist, writing in the *Sunday Herald:*

> A police surveillance team believed two of the suspected bombers lived in the block, one of them Hussein Osman.

Among the surveillance team in Scotia Road was a soldier from a new 'special forces' regiment that had only become operational in April. The Special Reconnaissance Regiment (SRR) is the first special forces unit to be created in the UK since the end of the second world war. The SRR is based in Hereford, its personnel selected and trained by the SAS. Geoff Hoon, then defence secretary, announced on April 5 in a written Commons answer that 'the pursuit of international terrorists' would be the SRR's priority.

However, the involvement of the SRR in the operation on July 22 was not confined to just one soldier at Scotia Road. According to security sources, SRR personnel were involved in the tailing operation that saw de Menezes leave the block of flats, board a bus, and then enter the tube station at Stockwell . . . The SRR soldier at Scotia Road (given the codename Tango 10) used equipment which sent realtime pictures of all who came and went from the flats. Those receiving the pictures could check them against footage of who they were looking for. One security source said: 'In this kind of operation you never leave. You need to pee: you use a bottle; if there's no bottle, tough. You never leave.'[30]

Questions arose. If Menezes was seriously suspected of being a suicide terrorist why was he allowed to board a bus? Why wasn't he confronted at the time? When he reached Stockwell Station, he pushed his pass through the barrier, picked up a copy of the London free newspaper *Metro*, and boarded the train. Why did the

---

[30] James Cusick, 'A Cover-Up? And If So . . . Why?', *Sunday Herald*, 21 August 2005. Cusick's report was better than anything I read in the London press.

surveillance team allow him to do so? Who authorized the special unit to board the train and kill Menezes? Was it Cressida Dick, the 'Gold Command' on duty that day? Her partisans leaked reports to suggest that she had given a firm instruction that he should be taken alive. If this is true, who countermanded her orders?

The execution itself was brutal. The shooters boarded the train and started firing even though Menezes had not offered any resistance as he was grabbed and pinioned by the surveillance team. One of their number was dragged to the ground by a colleague as eleven bullets were pumped into the target. There was continuous firing for thirty seconds. Who fired these bullets? According to James Cusick, 'A security agency source contacted by the *Sunday Herald* said: "This take-out is the signature of a special forces operation. It is not the way the police usually do things. We know members of SO19 have been receiving training from the SAS, but even so, this has special forces written all over it."'

Within hours of Menezes's death, Metropolitan Police Commissioner Sir Ian Blair addressed a press conference at Scotland Yard. His message was that Menezes was 'directly linked' to the anti-terrorist investigation. The Met press office spun the same line, now embroidered with some total fabrications. It was alleged that Menezes was dressed suspiciously for a summer's day, wearing a 'bulky coat' or padded jacket. False. He was wearing a light denim jacket, as the CCTV footage clearly revealed. It was alleged that he had fled from the police, jumping over the ticket barrier and running for the train. False. He walked calmly and was seated reading a newspaper when his killers pounced on him. There were further allegations about his visa having run out, presumably leaked to mobilize hostility towards an 'illegal immigrant' who had escaped Clarke's or Blunkett's net.

This false information was regurgitated by the *Evening Standard* the same evening, and by the rest of the press the following day, producing some exemplary *Pravda*-style 'supportive' headlines. 'Bomber Shot Dead on the Tube', declared the *Standard*. 'One Down, Three to Go', gloated the *Sun*. These were followed by a spate of editorials in favour of 'shoot to kill'—the *Guardian*, *Observer* and *Independent on Sunday* all hewing to the *Financial Times* line of seeking 'consensus' with government and, above all, avoiding any 'demonstrations of independence'.

It took twenty-four hours for Scotland Yard to admit that the dead man was not connected to the suicide bombings or to any other anti-terrorism operation. It took another four hours—9.30 pm on 23 July—before they released Menezes's name. Interestingly enough it was the conservative *Daily Telegraph* and *Daily Mail* who, while expressing support for the police and its dilemmas, raised some tough-minded questions. In contrast, at the liberal end of the spectrum, the *Guardian* in two successive editorials over a week first backed the shoot-to-kill policy and then delivered a rapturous encomium for the police:

> People seem to have decided that the police can make
> a dreadful mistake and yet still be worthy of support

at the same time. A week after the innocent Brazilian was killed, an immense collective effort to identify and capture the real criminals appeared to have harvested spectacular success last night. This could not have happened if the police were not good at their job—no wonder their ratings have rocketed. But that in turn could not have happened without public support and, in particular, support from the very communities whose trust in our institutions was supposedly most in doubt. None of it would have been possible if the police had not planted seeds of trust long before the first bombers arrived at King's Cross on the morning of July 7.[31]

Compare this to the *Daily Telegraph*'s position on 25 July 2005:

For someone who obviously takes public relations seriously, Sir Ian Blair, the Metropolitan Police Commissioner, has a marked tendency to use unfortunate phrases. An hour before the bombs went off on July 7, he was telling the Today programme that his force 'set

---

[31] *Guardian*, 30 July 2005. If chief leader writer Martin Kettle carries on in this vein, the readership will haemorrhage fast. News coverage in the *Guardian* has already declined drastically; there is hardly any investigative journalism and foreign news is largely derivative (a rare excption being Gary Younge's reports from the US). Where there is still some reflection of the traditions of a once proudly radical paper is in its Comment pages (constantly under attack from the Blair brigade). These pages are consistently more diverse than any of their equivalents in the US, Australia or elsewhere in Britain—not to speak of *Le Monde*, *La Repubblica* or *Suddeutsche Zeitung*. If the Comment pages are neutered there would no longer be any reason to read the *Guardian*.

the gold standard in counter-terrorism'. A week later, he announced that his officers were 'very tired men and women, but they've got big grins'—an odd thing to say in the aftermath of the carnage. Now, in seeking to explain why Jean Charles de Menezes, a man unconnected to the terrorists, was pinned down and shot five times in the back of the head, he says that the 'underlying cause' of Mr de Menezes's death was not police action.

Sir Ian is, of course, in a difficult position. These are not normal times: different standards apply to potential suicide bombers than to thieves and muggers. Shooting to disable is not an option when dealing with someone who is eager to immolate those around him. Nor do we know all the details surrounding Mr de Menezes's death. But, bearing all this in mind, it seems strange that the police allowed a man they suspected of being a bomber to leap in to a crowded Tube carriage in the first place. It is understandable, indeed laudable, that Sir Ian should want to stand by his officers; and no one doubts that the policemen acted in good faith. But what purpose was served by announcing, six hours after the shooting, that the dead man had been 'directly linked' to the investigation?

While for the *Daily Mail* on 30 July:

What is even more worrying is the growing suspicion that the authorities are reluctant to tell us the full truth about this terrible affair.

For instance, was it really necessary for the Home Office to leak news that Mr Menezes had a fake visa, as though his offence somehow mitigates this tragedy? But then, from the very beginning, there has been disingenuity over this blunder. The unfortunate Mr Menezes was not 'directly linked' with anti-terror operations, as Metropolitan Police chief Sir Ian Blair assured us at the time.

He just emerged from a building linked with the suspects and was followed by police for two miles before they shot him. Why did they allow him to board a bus, if they thought he was a bomber? Why claim he was wearing a heavy winter coat on a warm day—one sign of a potential suicide attacker—when they told his family he had only a lightweight denim jacket? Why was it claimed he had vaulted the barrier at Stockwell Tube station, when it now seems he did no such thing?

Why don't police release the CCTV film if he was really acting suspiciously? Why allow him anywhere near the Tube anyway? Did they shout a warning? Why weren't Parliament or the public told about the new rules on shoot to kill?

But public unease over the response to the terrorist threat doesn't stop with this one ghastly mistake. If Britain is to regain the moral high ground on the war on terror and repair some of the damage inflicted on the police reputation abroad, it is essential that there is clarity, transparency and truth over Mr Menezes.

The problem is that over Iraq, Mr Blair is in denial. His repeated insistence that the invasion had nothing to do with the London bombings is simply preposterous.

Of course, Iraq is not the only cause. But to deny it has anything to do with terrorism hardly inspires confidence in his conduct of the campaign against terror.

Now Britain faces Draconian new emergency powers that threaten to dilute our traditional freedoms.

Yet whatever the arguments for curtailing liberty in the cause of security we have so far not seen the unsparing honesty from politicians or police chiefs that we are entitled to expect in a crisis.

An Independent Police Complaints Commission inquiry into the tragedy of Menezes's death is under way, working to the usual slow-motion schedule of such investigations which are tacitly expected not to report until the whole affair has all but disappeared from public memory. The extent of the IPCC's appetite for uncovering the facts remains to be seen. On 16 August a whistle blower, clearly troubled by the slowness with which things were moving, leaked documents from the IPCC inquiry to ITV. It was these that stated that Menezes had been wearing a denim jacket, did not leap the ticket barrier, etc.—demolishing Sir Ian Blair and the Met's claims. The leaks were met with silence from Downing Street while the *Guardian*, aware of the history of fudges and cover-ups with anything involving the police, denounced the whistleblower:

> There are always two questions that should be asked about any leaked document. One is what it contains. The other is what the leaker hopes to achieve . . . it would have been better if the dramatic details of the Independent Police Complaints Commission's investigation into the shooting of Jean Charles de Menezes had not been leaked. They should have been allowed to emerge in the full report, based on all the evidence, which the IPCC is currently drawing up . . . Those who want justice to be done, as opposed to those with other agendas, must be careful.[32]

Other agendas? What did the chief leader writer mean? In fact the leaks had brought the truth out into the open

---

[32] *Guardian*, 18 August 2005.

and Sir Ian Blair was forced to retreat. To support one Blair uncritically is bad enough. To support them both suggests an agenda—that of the government–media consensus promoted by the *FT* triumvirs after the Hutton whitewash of Blair and Campbell's role in Kelly's death. The tone of all these embedded journalists is remarkably similar: pious yet spiteful, simultaneously servile and authoritarian.

'In good faith': the loyal media put the phrase into circulation whenever the state has been caught out lying or killing. The executioners carried out their task 'in good faith'; an even greater, blinder faith is demanded from the rest of us. What is needed in these scoundrel times is a combative, creative, critical journalism, but the dominant culture has too much to lose from this— not least, the shredding of that web of falsehood and obfuscation that surrounds its policy in Iraq.

It appears that what took place on July 22nd was that, once a 'suspect' had been identified, a premeditated execution was ordered, probably carried out by an SAS unit, experts in these matters. But why? As a deterrent in a country where capital punishment is forbidden? It can merely deter dark-skinned people from travelling on the Underground. Those who are prepared to sacrifice their own lives are unlikely to be put off by this. And what if Hussain Osman or one of his Muslim friends had been the victim? Would that have provoked any fuss at all? It should be stressed, as none of the mainstream papers have, that that too would have been wrong; both legally and morally unacceptable.

One of the apologists for the shoot-to-kill policy is the former head of Scotland Yard, John Stevens. Now a peer of the realm, he boasted that it was he who had set this policy in place in the aftermath of 9/11.[33] He appears to have learnt nothing from his stint in Northern Ireland during the 'troubles'. Stevens was sent to investigate the shoot-to-kill policies of the British Army, RUC and extremist Protestant paramilitary groups, and found strong evidence of collusion between the three groups to kill Irish nationalists. Has he forgotten the impact of those killings in the Catholic communities of Northern Ireland? If not, why is he defending similar actions in mainland Britain? When the state uses terror in this fashion it unleashes a parallel response. The cycle of violence continues until a political solution is found. It may take a long time, as in Ireland, but it is the only route. For Blair to accept this, however, would imply a radical change in the foreign policy that Powell so crudely yet aptly outlined to Meyer in 1997: staying up Washington's posterior.

---

[33] Shoot to kill is not a new policy for SAS and other units. It was enforced during the Irish war and it led to innocents' deaths in those years as well. In 1988 three IRA members were shot dead in Gibraltar. They were accused of having a bomb in their car—a story flagged by the entire media, but which turned out to be false. Thames TV, an independent broadcaster, proved conclusively that the entire operation was a set-up and that the IRA volunteers had been unarmed. When *This Week* broadcast these results from its investigation, the dam broke. The print media reluctantly followed suit. Thatcher never forgot this 'demonstration of independence' and Thames TV's franchise was removed at the next opportunity.

6

The War Against Civil Liberties

Anglo-Saxon politicians have a tendency to mouth the same rhetoric in the face of terror attacks. One particular mantra—shrouded in untruth—is constantly repeated: 'We shall not permit these attacks to change our way of life.' One purpose of this is to convince the public that, rather than having any political motivation that might have been caused by imperialist policies, the terrorists are crazed fundamentalists bent on destroying democracy, modernity, 'our values', etc.

The reason it constitutes a falsehood is because the attacks have, precisely, been used by our governments to change 'our way of life'. The Patriot Act in the United States and the measures either implemented or proposed by Blair in Britain demonstrate this quite clearly. As Alan Bennett puts it in his play, *The History Boys*, the message is that it's necessary to curb civil liberties for the sake of freedom. Senior lawyers of every political persuasion have argued that what we are witnessing is a concerted attack on civil rights that far outstrips anything implemented by Thatcher or Major. The New Labour government, they say, is qualitatively worse than the Conservatives.

What is being proposed in Britain is the indefinite suspension of habeas corpus. Worried by the recent judicial activism with unlikely senior judges in Britain expressing a real concern at the growing attack on civil liberties, Tony Blair warned them in public that he would brook no dissent, threatening that 'the rules of the game have changed'. But the legal and judicial system is not a game. Blair had been angered, a few months previously, by a statement from Lord Hoffmann, one of Britain's senior judges, who had stated bluntly that the laws being proposed by the government to curb civil liberties would inflict more damage to the fabric of British society than terrorism. What we are witnessing is a new round of repression by a reactionary government determined to dodge the fact that the recent wave of violence in London was provoked by its own disastrous policies in Iraq, Afghanistan and the Middle East. Laws designed to permit 'preventive detention', regularly used to maintain imperial domination in the colonies, have now returned home. As Blair explained in an August 2005 statement on the government's new measures:

> Should legal obstacles arise, we will legislate further, including, if necessary, amending the Human Rights Act, in respect of the interpretation of the ECHR. In any event, we will consult on legislating specifically for a non-suspensive appeal process in respect of deportations.
>
> One other point on deportations. Once the new grounds take effect, there will be a list drawn up of specific extremist websites, bookshops, centres, networks and particular organisations of concern. Active engagement with any of these will be a trigger for the home secretary to consider the deportation of any foreign national.
>
> As has been stated already, there will be new anti-terrorism legislation in the autumn. This will include an

offence of condoning or glorifying terrorism. The sort of remarks made in recent days should be covered by such laws. But this will also be applied to justifying or glorifying terrorism anywhere, not just in the UK.[34]

Will the British Parliament accept this view and legislate in favour of the new authoritarianism? In the absence of an opposition either outside the Labour Party or inside it, and given the climate of fear perpetrated by Blair, Blunkett, Clarke and the rest, the question is barely worth asking. We have already seen how the Labour Party has been reduced to a political corpse, barely capable of lifting a finger against the government's atrocities. The few decent Labour MPs prepared to do so cannot gain any traction inside a parliamentary party whose membership has largely been hand-picked by the leadership.

As for the Conservatives, they have yet to recover from Thatcher's deadly legacy. Though the Blairites stole the political clothes of the defeated Tories in 1997, the vanquished were permitted to retain their bovver boots. That was all the public ever saw. Trying to denounce Labour from the right on issues such as immigration and asylum seekers makes them sound like sympathizers of the BNP. Michael Howard, Tory leader at the time of writing, is a third-rate politician with a second-rate mind. He has both accused Blair of inconsistencies and demanded even tougher measures.

---

[34] See Appendix Three for a complete text of Blair's statement.

In reality Howard, like David Cameron, David Davis and most of this wretched and ineffective bunch, is little more than Blair's echo chamber.[35]

Characteristically, Howard joined Blair in denouncing the 2004 ruling of the Law Lords (the closest Britain has to a Supreme Court) that the indefinite detention without trial of foreign terror suspects under the 2001 Anti-Terrorism Act contravened the Human Rights Act. Lord Steyn had argued that the suspension of Article 5, 'so that people can be locked up without trial when there is no evidence on which they could be prosecuted, is not in the present circumstances justified.' In defence of Blair, the so-called Leader of the Opposition argued:

> Parliament must be supreme. Aggressive judicial activism will not only undermine the public's confidence in the impartiality of our judiciary. It could also put our security at risk—and with it the freedoms the judges seek to defend. That would be a price we cannot be expected to pay.[36]

---

[35] Credit should go to the handful of Conservatives who have put up a fight. On 1 September 2005 Ken Clarke, a long-serving member of Thatcher's Cabinet, denounced the government for going to war in Iraq, insisted that the London bombings were linked to that war and argued that further encroachments on civil liberties at home and the use of outsourced torture were unjustifiable. On 3 September, Max Hastings, former editor of the *Daily Telegraph*, writing in the *Guardian*, criticized Straw's refusal to face reality: 'It is equally absurd to deny that British support for American Iraq policy has made this country more vulnerable to terrorism, as many of us said it would.'

[36] *Daily Telegraph*, 10 August 2005.

Here again there is a blank refusal to accept what really puts 'security at risk'. The identical views of the neo-con Blairites and the Tory leadership is an indication of the current crisis of representation. The corrupt first-past-the-post electoral system has now become a serious threat to democratic functioning in Britain. In 2005, as I've pointed out, Blair was re-elected by less than 22 per cent of the overall electorate—the lowest percentage secured by any governing party in recent European history. According to several opinion polls, a majority of the population opposed the war in Iraq; a majority of the population favours withdrawing British troops; 66 per cent believe that the attacks on London were linked to Blair's decision to send troops to Iraq (this is also the view of sections of the Establishment).

Many measures proposed were tried during the years of the Irish 'troubles', from shoot-to-kill to deport-at-will; special courts sanctioned imprisonment without trial, etc. But judges were more reliable in those days and unhampered by European Human Rights legislation. That is why Blair is proposing that judges who try Muslim suspects should themselves be security-vetted. In other words, files will be opened to determine their reliability.

Laws openly regarded as unjust by large sections of the population usually fail on every front. They do not act as a deterrent and they weaken the legitimacy of the state. A law that is crudely manipulated to serve the interests of a particular class or maintain an insecure government in power (one, for instance, that is elected by barely a fifth of the voters) ceases to be effective. The

71

struggle against corrupt and repressive laws has a long pedigree in English history. Though the eighteenth- and nineteenth-century poor had long experience of the fact that most of the laws in force were exclusively designed to protect property and privilege, they fought for justice when even these laws were transgressed in an arbitrary fashion.[37] Today, hard-won rights need to be defended against the Labour government's attempts to weaken and abolish them.

In 2004, Helena Kennedy, QC gave a lecture at the Bath Festival of Literature on 'New Labour and the Law'.[38] Listening to her in a packed hall with six hundred others, I was shocked by my own failure to have registered how liberties hitherto taken for granted were being whittled away without any serious opposition in parliament, the media or the country at large. The jury system had, for many centuries, been the only hope of the poor brought before a magistrate. Records from the 1720s showed how many juries had refused to convict the poor despite the fact that they were in breach of the

---

[37] See, for instance, E. P. Thompson, *Whigs and Hunters: The Origins of the Black Act*, New York 1975, and the same author's *Customs In Common*, London 1991.

[38] With the death of the political parties, literary festivals in Britain have become a new focus for political discussion and debate. These events are often very well attended—much more so than Labour or Tory gatherings. For many people, these are the only political debates where they can question the speakers at length. The question-and-answer sessions are often more invigorating than anything inside the political-media bubble.

Black Act, which sent poachers on private land straight to the gallows. The jury system is now under attack from Labour, one of the excuses being that it is becoming too expensive.

There were urgent questions from the audience. The one that dominated the discussion was, 'What can I do to stop this?' With both the major political parties pledged to the further destruction of civil liberties, Kennedy had no easy answer. Nor did I. That same week I bought and read her book, *Just Law*, a longer version of the frightening case she had put before the audience in Bath. Kennedy had accused Blair of a serial onslaught on 'our liberties', much graver than anything attempted by his immediate predecessor. What was clear was that the draconian measures in place long before July 7th had done nothing to prevent the terrorist acts. Kennedy provides the following catalogue of Labour's record:

- Internment without trial for non-citizens suspected of terrorist links.

- Repeated efforts to reduce trial by jury for citizens on a whole range of issues.

- Retrial of those who have been acquitted, thus eroding the double jeopardy principle.

- Attacks on the independence of the judiciary.

- Serious limits on access to justice through cuts to legal aid.

- Abandonment of safeguards for accused people—increasingly placing previous convictions before juries, lowering the burden of proof (as in Anti-

Social Behaviour Orders) and shifting the burden of proof onto the accused.

- Severe limitation on the right to silence.

- Imprisonment of more people for longer.

- 'Pre-emptive strike' incarceration of the mentally ill.

- Special punishments for the poor.

- Neighbourhood curfews against young people.

- Huge expansion in the powers of the state to invade privacy.

- Subversion of new technology such as telecommunications and DNA for undeclared ends.

- Streamlining of extradition processes so that British citizens can be removed abroad with insufficient protections.

- Incitement of public fear of terrorism, crime, asylum seekers, immigrants and paedophiles to justify serious erosions of civil liberty.

- Introduction of identity cards so that people can be monitored all times.

- Removal of judicial review in asylum cases.[39]

---

[39] Helena Kennedy, *Just Law*, London 2004. There used to be an organization in Britain known as the National Council of Civil Liberties, which changed its name to Liberty. Two of its leading members—Patricia Hewitt and Harriet Harman— were fierce defenders of the law and campaigned hard against its infringements in the case of Irish prisoners and other civilians. And now? As members of the Labour government, Hewitt and Harman have unbroken records of support for the catalogue detailed above. We need an organization like the NCCL again—an angry campaigning body, not a lobbyist.

The roots of the modern jury system lie in the assizes created by Henry II to settle property disputes between landowners. The defendant in the case had a choice between assizes consisting of his peers—twelve good knights and true who had to return a unanimous verdict—or trial by combat. (New Labour could consider reviving the trial by combat: Dyke v Hutton, Abu Qatada v Blunkett, etc.)

Eighteen months after Kennedy had outlined her case against Blair, another Labour veteran, Roy Hattersley, shocked by a particularly crass statement of Blair's on criminal justice, wrote a public *mea culpa*:

Last Friday, after a contrived photo opportunity at the Beechwood Family Centre in Watford—regulation mug of tea in hand—he described one of his aspirations for a better Britain. It was a 'historic shift from a criminal justice system which asks: "how do we protect the accused from the transgressions of the state and police?" to one whose first question is "How do we protect the majority from the dangerous and irresponsible minority?"'

Could any grown man—with even a smattering of understanding about the real world—genuinely imagine that the criminal justice system is based on the principle that its primary purpose is the protection of suspected criminals against the law? Does the prime minister really believe that an obligation to hamstring the police was the imperative that motivated MPs as they passed successive bills in the last parliament? Was it the hope that guided David Blunkett when he was home secretary? Is it the principle that judges observe when they administer the law, and the aim of every voluntary justice of the peace who sacrifices valuable leisure time in order to sit on the local bench?

The criminal justice system should certainly contain safeguards against the conviction of innocent men and women, and it is possible to argue about whether or not, at present, those safeguards are too weak or too strong. But the suggestion that the protection of 'transgressors' is the basis of our present system is balderdash. And the prime minister must know that to be so.[40]

Then there is the torture. In a Western world saturated with talk on human rights (and with carefully vetted journalists occupying so many chairs in the subject on US campuses), it is noticeable how few influential voices have been raised against the 'democratic' torture practices of the West. A courageous but tiny band of writers, journalists and lawyers have produced strong denunciations; but in Britain, many good citizens shrug their shoulders and blame it on the United States. But what of the British security services's participation in the network of torture centres run by the US, in Afghanistan and elsewhere? What of the interrogations they have carried out in Guantanamo? Torture is banned in Cuba proper. Even Castro's worst enemies have not been able to provide any evidence of it in Cuban prisons. The only torture on the island takes place in the US military base.

The testimonies of three innocent young men from Tipton in the West Midlands—captured in Afghanistan by a warlord of the Northern Alliance, put in a container and taken by US soldiers to a military prison and

---

[40] Roy Hattersley, 'The danger in Blair's balderdash', *Guardian*, 5 September 2005.

then transferred to Guantanamo—should be compulsory reading for every member of parliament. The Blair government is thoroughly complicit in the interrogations that take place in Camp X-Ray. The three men from Tipton were threatened and interrogated by MI5 while shackled and hung from hooks. All three of them told their lawyer, Gareth Pierce, that MI5 'was content to benefit from the effect of the isolation, sleep deprivation and other forms of acutely painful and degrading treatment'.[41] Why don't even a handful of British members of parliament demand an investigation and refuse to take 'national security concerns prevent us from answering your question' as an answer?

'Oh, may no more a foreign master's rage / With wrongs yet legal, curse a future age!' wrote Alexander Pope. Three centuries later, we have Guantanamo, Abu Ghraib and Britain's very own state security prison, Belmarsh, in South East London. The official spin at Belmarsh is typically New Labour: the 'regime includes education, workshops, farms & gardens and training courses, including Enhanced Thinking Skills, Substance Awareness and Anger Management'. The reality was starkly different for the sixteen men who were arrested in December 2001 and taken either to Belmarsh or to Woodhill Prison, near Milton Keynes. They were to be held indefinitely without trial at the government's pleasure.

---

[41] 'Detention in Afghanistan and Guantanamo Bay', statement of Shafiq Rasul, Asif Iqbal and Rhuhel Ahmed. Unpublished document.

All these men were refugees who had been granted asylum. Some of them had been brutally tortured in their own country. They were arrested under the post-9/11 Anti-Terrorism Crime and Security Act. It was internment without trial once again, contravening Britain's European Treaty obligations. Gareth Peirce, the prisoners' solicitor, explained the circumstances in which Home Secretary Blunkett had pushed through the law:

In December 2001, two years ago, our Home Secretary informed the Council of Europe that there was in the UK a national emergency threatening the life of the nation so extreme that the UK needed to withdraw from its treaty obligation, specifically the obligation that no individual could be detained without trial. No other country of the now 40-plus member states of Europe has felt that necessity. At the beginning, when the Home Secretary announced the legislation that he was intending, he was reminded that it was impermissible short of a national emergency. His response was that that was a 'technicality'.

Later, clearly after having forceful legal advice, he attempted to put flesh on the bone of that claim. The claim that was then made was that there was a specific threat of a kind only encountered otherwise in a time of war or internal armed conflict and that came from al Qaeda and organisations and individuals closely linked to and working in harmony with al Qaeda with the same objectives, the objective being to attack America and its close allies, Israel and the United Kingdom.

The word internment still was equated in the public memory with injustice after mass internment of a significant percentage of half of the population of Northern Ireland, more than 30 years ago. It had been a disaster.

It had failed to incarcerate IRA activists. The so-called intelligence on which it was based was entirely erroneous and the burning injustice had the effect of consolidating support for armed struggle for more than three decades against those who had imposed it.[42]

Three years later, on 21 August 2005, in her appeal for bail, Gareth Peirce told the Special Immigration Appeals Commission that:

The mental and physical breakdown of a number of the detainees during the course of the three years of detention under the 2001 Act of course had significant effect upon them as individuals (and for those who were married, their families also), but in turn had a marked effect upon the small group of detainees as a whole also subject to the same legislation. Those individuals found it incumbent upon them (and indeed volunteered as a moral obligation) to provide care, both mentally and physically, for those who were disabled and who became ill.

The first of the detainees to deteriorate sharply into florid mental breakdown was Mahmoud Abu Rideh, a Palestinian with refugee status in this country. (Mr Abu Rideh has not been made the subject of the current deportation orders; he does not, of course, have a country to which he could be deported. He remains at home, the subject of a Control Order, in constant touch with his lawyers and psychiatrists, indicating that he is too terrified to attempt any normality of existence, believing that he too may well be about to be the subject of arbitrary rearrest.)

In the summer of 2002, Mahmoud Abu Rideh was transferred by the Secretary of State to Broadmoor

---

[42] Gareth Peirce, 'Talk on Internment', 15 December 2003. Unpublished.

Hospital. Thereafter two others of those currently detained also came to be transferred to Broadmoor (in late 2004). Those were Mustafa Melke, a double amputee suffering by then from severe depression and paranoia and Mohamed Boutemine. (The Home Office jointly instructed a psychiatrist with Mr Melke's solicitors; there was no disagreement as to the high risk accompanying any continued detention of Mr Melke in prison; he too was therefore transferred to Broadmoor Hospital.)

What had reduced these men to this state? Clearly they had been subjected to psychological torture, just like the Irish prisoners during the 'troubles.' One should never underestimate the sadism of specialist interrogaters. Gerry Adams—Sinn Fein President and MP for West Belfast—had felt obliged to remind us at the time of the Abu Ghraib revelations how torture had been a systematic component of British rule in Ireland. Adams described how he had been physically and psychologically brutalized:

> I have been arrested a few times and interrogated on each occasion by a mixture of RUC or British army personnel. The first time was in Palace Barracks in 1972. I was placed in a cubicle in a barracks-style wooden hut and made to face a wall of boards with holes in it, which had the effect of inducing images, shapes and shadows. There were other detainees in the rest of the cubicles. Though I didn't see them I could hear the screaming and shouting. I presumed they got the same treatment as me, punches to the back of the head, ears, small of the back, between the legs. From this room, over a period of days, I was taken back and forth to interrogation rooms.

> On these journeys my captors went to very elabo-
> rate lengths to make sure that I saw nobody and that no
> one saw me. I was literally bounced off walls and into
> doorways. Once I was told I had to be fingerprinted, and
> when my hands were forcibly outstretched over a table, a
> screaming, shouting and apparently deranged man in a
> blood-stained apron came at me armed with a hatchet.
>
> Another time my captors tried to administer what
> they called a truth drug.
>
> Once a berserk man came into the room yelling and
> shouting. He pulled a gun and made as if he was trying
> to shoot at me while others restrained him.[43]

We do not yet have the details of how the Muslim prisoners in Belmarsh have been tortured. Those driven
mad have perhaps lost the ability to convey what they
went through, but the same does not apply to liberal
public opinion. It is much safer and easier to denounce
torture in Guantanamo. Bush and Cheney are soft targets. What of Blair and Blunkett, Hewitt and Harman,
Goldsmith and Reid? Evidence obtained under torture
in Guantanamo, an MI5 witness informed the Appeals
Tribunal in London, had been used in the case of the
Belmarsh prisoners. How many members of parliament
rose to question Blair or his ministers on the ordeal
being suffered by political prisoners in Britain? How
many journalists of integrity and courage seriously
investigated the conditions that led from Belmarsh
to Broadmoor?

---

[43] Gerry Adams, 'I have been in torture photos, too', *Guardian*,
5 June 2004. For the benefit of those with short memory spans I
have included the Adams text as Appendix Two.

In some ways there was more dissent and anger in nineteenth-century England. It was not only Shelley who denounced Lord Castlereagh after Peterloo. A whole string of radical pamphleteers and journalists kept watch. In 1818 a totally innocent man, Frank Ward, a Nottingham lace manufacturer, was accused of having planned an insurrection in Derbyshire. The calumny was repeated endlessly in the *Observer* newspaper. Ward was arrested and charged. After he had been acquitted by a jury, the editor of the *Black Dwarf*, Thomas Wooler, in an open letter to Castlereagh, documented how Ward had been framed and in a stinging attack on repression, also referred to the pro-government journalists of the day:

> Your minions, throughout the empire, are of the same materials and entertain the same feelings, as yourself, and Oliver, and Sidmouth . . . They possess, therefore, by instinct, your antipathy to honesty and independence: and when the cry of BLOOD was raised by the huntsmen of the treasury, the bloodhounds fastened on all who could be deemed obnoxious to the reptiles there.[44]

One reason for the indifference shown by liberal opinion to the Muslim prisoners is that their politics are regarded to be repugnant. But this is a recent development. Some of the prisoners were once allies of the West as they fought the jihad against the Soviet Union in Afghanistan; others fought alongside the United

---

[44] Thomas Wooler, 'On the Triumph of Frank Ward', *Black Dwarf*, 20 January 1819.

States against the Serbs in Bosnia; a few were involved in the Chechen independence struggle. My own politics are totally removed from those of the prisoners—or of the more moderate versions of Islamism cultivated by Blair—but that is irrelevant. What we have is a gross violation of civil liberties: torture and imprisonment without trial. The implication of this is that there is no evidence against these men that would be admissible in any ordinary court of law. This is unacceptable.

In the aftermath of July 7th, Blair has been announcing his intention to deport a large number of foreign nationals, including some of these prisoners, back to Algeria, Jordan and Egypt. Since it would be in contravention of European law to do so if there was a likelihood of their being tortured in these countries, the Labour government will demand assurances from the governments concerned, in order to cover iself before the European Court. One can imagine the hollow laughter from prisoners already held in those countries' jails.

These means are supposed to be justified by the ends of isolating and marginalizing terror networks, and sealing them off from new recruits. But torture won't help today any more than it did with the Irish. Then, as now, one has to go to the roots of the problem: Iraq and Palestine, where Israeli soldiers also 'shoot to kill' and where the daily humiliation and suffering inflicted on the population remind one of the darkest days of European colonialism. But 'Israel has no closer friend than this government' bleats the Prime Minister. Another falsehood, of course. Britain can hardly compete with the United States in the scale of its support—military, economic or political—for Israel. Israeli leaders are compelled to listen and obey on the few occasions when the White House has cracked the whip; under Bush Snr, for example. They merely laugh at Blair.

7

Conclusions

What, then, is to be done? There is one immediate and several medium-term steps that need to be taken to solve this crisis.

First, Britain must withdraw its troops from Iraq and Afghanistan. It should do so not because it is under terrorist pressure, but because these interventions were wrong in the first place.

Secondly, there needs to be a moratorium on state sponsorship of religion. Blair and his Cabinet have avidly fostered single-faith schools. Over one-third of British state schools are religious and the National Secular Society has published figures that reveal Labour permitting forty more non-religious state secondaries be taken over by the Church of England in the last four years, with another 54 about to go. Given this situation, it is impossible to deny the same rights to other religions. Matters are not helped by the fact that Blair's Opus Dei Education Secretary has stressed that the 'bombs' will not stop her encouraging the formation of more single-faith schools. Wonderful.

What is required is a high-quality state education system that provides the same education to rich and poor, Christian, Hindu, Jewish, Muslim or non-religious children. Religion should be taught as comparative history. If parents want a religious education as well, they are perfectly free to send their children to special Sunday schools under the control of mosque, church or synagogue.

Meanwhile, 'good' Muslims are being paraded on TV arguing that violence is not advocated in the Koran and therefore the bombers are wrong. The implication here is that, if the Koran permitted them, such actions it would be fine. In fact, as is well-known, there are different readings of the Koran, both pacifist and violent, depending on your mood. The Old Testament, in contrast, has no passages in praise of peace. Revenge, torture and rape are all available here. What if some young Muslims convert to the oldest and purest monotheist faith and start to implement the prescription contained therein? Establishing a religious criterion is, in these circumstances, counter-productive.

Thirdly, Britain needs to quit its role as automated adjutant to Washington's neo-imperialism and develop a rational, independent foreign policy. A central plank of this must be an economically, politically and militarily viable Palestinian state, with full state rights. The linkage to the US-Israeli expansionist project in the Middle East has been a disaster not just for Britain but for the whole region, Israel included. Anglo-American governments' build up of Islamic fundamentalism in Pakistan, Afghanistan and elsewhere in the 1980s has produced a catastrophe; they have learnt nothing from it. Now they have launched a war against Islamism that is producing an even greater catastrophe—and still they are incapable of learning from it.

Fourthly, we need a re-launched campaign in defence of civil liberties that can really mobilise, actively and effectively, the hundreds of thousands who are appalled by the new (provenly ineffective) anti-terror laws—laws that are permitting detention without trial and the types of torture inflicted on the Belmarsh detainees.

Fifthly, the paralysis within parliament needs to be overcome. Atavistic political structures have insulated the government from public opinion. The first-past-the-post electoral system precludes democratic functioning. We need a system of proportional representation for electing the House of Commons. Blair's cynical dismissal of the pledge on proportional representation in the 1997 Labour Manifesto should not be forgiven or forgotten. The House of Lords should either be abolished or replaced by an elected chamber representing the different regional and national components of Britain. Labour's reform of the House of Lords has been the constitutional equivalent of a Michael Jackson face-lift.

More broadly, the latest phase of capitalism has constricted and truncated political life—especially, but not only, in the old heartlands of capital. Politics is concentrated economics and nowhere is this more explicit than in the United States. Here the link between big money and politics has corrupted the whole system, creating a new form of power. Sheldon Wolin puts it succinctly:

> It is not only that the state and corporation have become partners; in the process, each has begun to mimic functions historically identified with the other. How does one describe the 'power' of a corporation such as Lockheed that once was engaged solely in the manufacture of

aircraft but now also operates publicly funded welfare programmes? Old-fashioned economic power may have enabled Lockheed to offer politicians the inducements necessary to procure contacts/contracts for its welfare operations, but a new mix of power and authority results from it.[45]

This new authority is fundamentally opposed to mass-democratic political activity. To be a good and loyal citizen you should be an individualist to the core, motivated primarily by competitiveness and personal greed. You must learn calmly to accept the unjust structures that institutionalize inequality. And, yes, it would be helpful if you also understood that all the wars fought by your state are designed to protect your interests.

It is only when citizens begin to break ranks on a critical issue that the unrepresentative nature of our 'representative democracies' is revealed. In the run-up to the Iraq War over a hundred city councils in the United States voted against the war. There was no reflection of this in the Senate and the House of Representatives. The million and a half who marched in London had less leverage over their members of parliament than did the Labour whips. In France and Holland, the citizens defeated their political and media establishments by rejecting the draft European Constitution in two successive referendums. The European establishment carried on as before. The Brazilian poor elected Lula as their President because he promised to improve their

---

[45] Sheldon Wolin, *Politics and Vision*, Princeton 2004, p. 588.

conditions. Instead he behaved like a kleptomaniac tropical Blair. This is why what is really called for in all these instances is a peasants' revolt.

Lastly, and sooner rather than later, we need a new political movement that can unite the swathe of opinion to the left of New Labour, building on the best elements of the radical and socialist traditions in this country and dumping the rest. There is no mainstream political party that speaks for the poor and the under-privileged in British society. This is a deficit that needs to be remedied.

Meanwhile it is time for Blair to go. A British colonel has been charged with committing crimes in Iraq. Were we to apply the norms of the Nuremberg War Crimes Tribunal, it would be the politicians who gave the orders and justified the invasion who would be in the dock. Blair once boasted that, in order to defeat Saddam Hussein, a 'blood price would have to be paid'. It has been paid, by tens of thousands of Iraqi dead and now by dozens of Londoners. There will be no peace as long as he remains Prime Minister.

APPENDIX ONE

Downing Street Memo on Iraq

SECRET AND STRICTLY PERSONAL – UK EYES ONLY

David Manning
From: Matthew Rycroft
Date: 23 July 2002
S 195/02

cc: Defence Secretary, Foreign Secretary, Attorney-General, Sir Richard Wilson, John Scarlett, Francis Richards, CDS, C, Jonathan Powell, Sally Morgan, Alastair Campbell

IRAQ: PRIME MINISTER'S MEETING, 23 JULY

Copy addressees and you met the Prime Minister on 23 July to discuss Iraq. This record is extremely sensitive. No further copies should be made. It should be shown only to those with a genuine need to know its contents.

John Scarlett summarised the intelligence and latest JIC assessment. Saddam's regime was tough and based on extreme fear. The only way to overthrow it was likely to be by massive military action. Saddam was worried and expected an attack, probably by air and land, but he was not convinced that it would be immediate or overwhelming. His regime expected their neighbours to line up with the US. Saddam knew that regular army morale was poor. Real support for Saddam among the public was probably narrowly based.

C reported on his recent talks in Washington. There was a perceptible shift in attitude. Military action was now seen as inevitable. Bush wanted to remove Saddam, through military action, justified by the conjunction of terrorism and WMD. But the intelligence and facts were being fixed around the policy. The NSC had no patience with the UN route, and no enthusiasm for publishing material on the Iraqi regime's record. There was little discussion in Washington of the aftermath after military action.

CDS said that military planners would brief CENTCOM on 1–2 August, Rumsfeld on 3 August and Bush on 4 August.

The two broad US options were:

(a) Generated Start. A slow build-up of 250,000 US troops, a short (72 hour) air campaign, then a move up to Baghdad from the south. Lead time of 90 days (30 days preparation plus 60 days deployment to Kuwait).

(b) Running Start. Use forces already in theatre (3 x 6,000), continuous air campaign, initiated by an Iraqi casus belli. Total lead time of 60 days with the air campaign beginning even earlier. A hazardous option.

The US saw the UK (and Kuwait) as essential, with basing in Diego Garcia and Cyprus critical for either option. Turkey and other Gulf states were also important, but less vital. The three main options for UK involvement were:

(i) Basing in Diego Garcia and Cyprus, plus three SF squadrons.

(ii) As above, with maritime and air assets in addition.

(iii) As above, plus a land contribution of up to 40,000, perhaps with a discrete role in Northern Iraq entering from Turkey, tying down two Iraqi divisions.

The Defence Secretary said that the US had already begun 'spikes of activity' to put pressure on the regime. No decisions had been taken, but he thought the most likely timing in US minds for military action to begin was January, with the timeline beginning 30 days before the US Congressional elections.

The Foreign Secretary said he would discuss this with Colin Powell this week. It seemed clear that Bush had made up his mind to take military action, even if the timing was not yet decided. But the case was thin. Saddam was not threatening his neighbours, and his WMD capability was less than that of Libya, North Korea or Iran. We should work up a plan for an ultimatum to Saddam to allow back in the UN weapons inspectors. This would also help with the legal justification for the use of force.

The Attorney-General said that the desire for regime change was not a legal base for military action. There were three possible legal bases: self-defence, humanitarian intervention, or UNSC authorisation. The first and second could not be the base in this case. Relying on UNSCR 1205 of three years ago would be difficult. The situation might of course change.

The Prime Minister said that it would make a big difference politically and legally if Saddam refused to allow in the UN inspectors. Regime change and WMD were linked in the sense that it was the regime that was producing the WMD. There were different strategies for dealing with Libya and Iran. If the political context were right, people would support regime change. The two key issues were whether the military plan worked and whether we had the political strategy to give the military plan the space to work.

On the first, CDS said that we did not know yet if the US battleplan was workable. The military were continuing to ask lots of questions.

For instance, what were the consequences, if Saddam used WMD on day one, or if Baghdad did not collapse and urban warfighting began? You said that Saddam could also use his WMD on Kuwait. Or on Israel, added the Defence Secretary.

The Foreign Secretary thought the US would not go ahead with a military plan unless convinced that it was a winning strategy. On this, US and UK interests converged. But on the political strategy, there could be US/UK differences. Despite US resistance, we should explore discreetly the ultimatum. Saddam would continue to play hard-ball with the UN.

John Scarlett assessed that Saddam would allow the inspectors back in only when he thought the threat of military action was real.

The Defence Secretary said that if the Prime Minister wanted UK military involvement, he would need to decide this early. He cautioned that many in the US did not think it worth going down the ultimatum route. It would be important for the Prime Minister to set out the political context to Bush.

Conclusions:

(a) We should work on the assumption that the UK would take part in any military action. But we needed a fuller picture of US planning before we could take any firm decisions. CDS should tell the US military that we were considering a range of options.

(b) The Prime Minister would revert on the question of whether funds could be spent in preparation for this operation.

Gerry Adams

I have been in torture photos, too

The Abu Ghraib images are all too familiar to Irish republicans

News of the ill-treatment of prisoners in Iraq created no great surprise in republican Ireland. We have seen and heard it all before. Some of us have even survived that type of treatment. Suggestions that the brutality in Iraq was meted out by a few miscreants aren't even seriously entertained here. We have seen and heard all that before as well. But our experience is that, while individuals may bring a particular impact to their work, they do so within interrogative practices authorised by their superiors.

For example, the interrogation techniques which were used following the internment swoops in the north of Ireland in 1971 were taught to the RUC by British military officers. Someone authorised this. The first internment swoops, 'Operation Demetrius', saw hundreds of people systematically beaten and forced to run the gauntlet of war dogs, batons and boots.

Some were stripped naked and had black hessian bags placed over their heads. These bags kept out all light and extended down over the head to the shoulders. As the men stood spread-eagled against the wall, their legs were kicked out from under them. They were beaten with batons and fists on the testicles and kidneys and kicked between the legs. Radiators and electric fires were placed under them as they were stretched over benches. Arms were twisted, fingers were twisted, ribs were pummelled, objects were shoved up the anus, they were burned with matches and treated to games of Russian roulette. Some of them were taken up in helicopters and flung out, thinking that they were high in the sky when they were only five or six feet off the ground. All the time they were hooded, handcuffed and subjected to a high-pitched unrelenting noise.

This was later described as extra-sensory deprivation. It went on for days. During this process some of them were photographed in the nude.

And although these cases ended up in Europe, and the British government paid thousands in compensation, it didn't stop the torture and ill-treatment of detainees. It just made the British government and its military and intelligence agencies more careful about how they carried it out and ensured that they changed the laws to protect the torturers and make it very difficult to expose the guilty.

I have been arrested a few times and interrogated on each occasion by a mixture of RUC or British army personnel. The first time was in Palace Barracks in 1972. I was placed in a cubicle in a barracks-style wooden hut and made to face a wall of boards with holes in it, which had the effect of inducing images, shapes and shadows. There were other detainees in the rest of the cubicles. Though I didn't see them I could hear the screaming and shouting. I presumed they got the same treatment as me, punches to the back of the head, ears, small of the back, between the legs. From this room, over a period of days, I was taken back and forth to interrogation rooms.

On these journeys my captors went to very elaborate lengths to make sure that I saw nobody and that no one saw me. I was literally bounced off walls and into doorways. Once I was told I had to be fingerprinted, and when my hands were forcibly outstretched over a table, a screaming, shouting and apparently deranged man in a blood-stained apron came at me armed with a hatchet.

Another time my captors tried to administer what they called a truth drug.

Once a berserk man came into the room yelling and shouting. He pulled a gun and made as if he was trying to shoot at me while others restrained him.

In between these episodes I was put up against a wall, spread-eagled and beaten soundly around the kidneys and up between the legs, on my back and on the backs of my legs. The beating was systematic and quite clinical. There was no anger in it.

During my days in Palace Barracks I tried to make a formal complaint about my ill-treatment. My interrogators ignored this and the uniformed RUC officers also ignored my demand when I was handed over to them. Eventually, however, I was permitted to make a formal complaint before leaving. But when I was taken to fill out a form I was confronted by a number of large baton-wielding redcaps who sought to dissuade me from complaining. I knew I was leaving so I ignored them and filled in the form.

Some years later I was arrested again, this time with some friends. We were taken to a local RUC barracks on the Springfield Road. There I was taken into a cell and beaten for what seemed to be an endless time. All the people who beat me were in plain clothes. They had English accents.

After the first initial flurry, which I resisted briefly, the beating became a dogged punching and kicking match with me as the punch bag. I was forced into the search position, palms against the walls, body at an acute angle, legs well spread. They beat me systematically. I fell to the ground. Buckets of water were flung over me. I was stripped naked. Once I was aroused from unconsciousness by a British army doctor. He seemed concerned about damage to my kidneys. After he examined me he left and the beatings began again. At one point a plastic bucket was placed over my head. I was left in the company of two uniformed British soldiers. I could see their camouflage trousers and heavy boots from beneath the rim of the bucket. One of them stubbed his cigarette out on my wrist. His mate rebuked him.

When the interrogators returned they were in a totally different mood and very friendly. I was given my clothes back, parts of them still damp. One of them even combed my hair. I could barely walk upright and I was very badly marked. In the barrack yard I was reunited with my friends and photographs were taken of us with our arresting party. For a short time other British soldiers, individually and in groups, posed beside us. Someone even videoed the proceedings.

We were to learn from all the banter that there was a bounty for the soldiers who captured us. According to them we were on an 'A' list, that is to be shot on sight. The various regiments kept a book which had accumulated considerable booty for whoever succeeded in apprehending us, dead or alive. From the craic in the barracks yard it was obvious that the lucky ones had won a considerable prize.

So for some time we were photographed in the company of young, noisy, exuberant squaddies. I'm sure we were not a pretty sight. I'm also sure that they were grinning as much as the soldiers in the photographs we have all seen recently. Our photos were never published, but somewhere, in some regimental museum or in the top of somebody's wardrobe or in the bottom of a drawer, there are photographs of me and my friends and our captors. To the victor, the spoils.

Guardian, 5 June 2004

The Prime Minister's
statement on anti-terror measures

Friday August 5, 2005

Since July 7 the response of the British people has been uni-fied, dignified and remarkable. Of course there is anxiety and worry. But the country knows the purpose of terrorism is to intimidate and it is not inclined to be intimidated. Of course too there have been isolated and unacceptable acts of a racial or religious hatred. But they have been isolated. By and large Britain knows it is a tolerant and good-natured nation, is rather proud of it and has responded to this terrorism with tolerance and good nature in a way that has won the admiration of people and nations the world over.

However, I am acutely aware that alongside these feelings is also a determination that this very tolerance and good nature should not be abused by a small, but fanatical minority; and an anger that it has been.

Time and again, over the past few weeks, I have been asked to deal firmly with those prepared to engage in such extrem-ism; and most particularly those who incite it or proselytise it. The Muslim community have been and are our partners in this endeavour. Much of the insistence on strong action to weed out extremism is coming most vigorously from Muslims them-selves, deeply concerned lest the activities of the fanatical fringe should contaminate the good reputation of the mainstream Muslim community in our country.

Such action in the past has been controversial. Each tight-ening of the law has met fierce opposition. Regularly we have had defeat in parliament or the courts. The anti-terrorism legislation, passed in 2002 after September 11 was declared partially invalid. The successor legislation hotly contested.

But, for obvious reasons, the mood now is different. People do not talk of "scaremongering". To be fair, the Conservative leadership has responded with a genuine desire to work together for the good of the country, as have the Liberal Democrats.

Over the past two weeks, intensive meetings across government have taken place to set a comprehensive framework for action in dealing with the terrorist threat in Britain. Today I want to give your our preliminary assessment of the measures we need urgently to examine.

In the meantime, insofar as administrative measures, not requiring legislation, can be taken, we will act with immediate effect.

In looking both at the law and administrative measures, we have surveyed extensively practice in other countries, including in particular other European countries. To assist this process, there will be a series of consultation papers over the coming weeks starting with a research paper that will detail experience in other countries. There will also be a cross government unit staffed by senior hand-picked officials to drive this forward under the guidance of Bill Jeffrey, the intelligence and security coordinator and the cabinet committee on counter terrorism which I chair. The home secretary with whom I have been talking closely in the past week, will have the cabinet responsibility for coordinating this.

Here are the measures either being taken now, immediately, or under urgent examination.

1.   The home secretary today publishes new grounds for deportation and exclusion. Deportation is a decision taken by the home secretary under statute. The new grounds will include fostering hatred, advocating violence to further a person's beliefs or justifying or validating such violence. These grounds will be subject to a short consultation period which will finish this

month. Even under existing grounds, however, we are today signalling a new approach to deportation orders. Let no one be in any doubt. The rules of the game are changing.

These issues will, of course, be tested in the courts. Up to now, the concern has been that orders for deportation will be struck down as contrary to article 3 of the ECHR [European convention on human rights], as interpreted by the European Court in the Chahal case in 1996; and indeed have had such cases struck down.

However, the circumstances of our national security have now self-evidently changed and we believe we can get the necessary assurances from the countries to which we will return the deportees, against their being subject to torture or ill-treatment contrary to article 3. We have concluded a Memorandum of Understanding with Jordan and are close to getting necessary assurances from other relevant countries. For example, just yesterday, I have had very constructive conversations with the leaders of Algeria and Lebanon. There are around 10 such countries with whom we are seeking such assurances.

France and Spain, to name just two other European countries, do deport by administrative decision. The effect is often immediate and in some cases the appeal is non-suspensive, in other words it takes place outside the country. The assurances given by the receiving nation are adequate for their courts and these countries are also subject to the ECHR and apply it directly.

So it is important to test this anew now, in view of the changed conditions in Britain. Should legal obstacles arise, we will legislate further, including, if necessary amending the Human Rights Act, in respect of the interpretation of the ECHR. In any event, we will consult on legislating specifically for a non-suspensive appeal process in respect of deportations.

101

One other point on deportations. Once the new grounds take effect, there will be a list drawn up of specific extremist websites, bookshops, centres, networks and particular organisations of concern. Active engagement with any of these will be a trigger for the home secretary to consider the deportation of any foreign national.

2. As has been stated already, there will be new anti-terrorism legislation in the autumn. This will include an offence of condoning or glorifying terrorism. The sort of remarks made in recent days should be covered by such laws. But this will also be applied to justifying or glorifying terrorism anywhere, not just in the UK.

3. Anyone who has participated in terrorism or has anything to do with it anywhere will automatically be refused asylum.

4. We have already powers to strip citizenship from those individuals with British or dual nationality who act in a way that is contrary to the interests of this country. We will now consult on extending these powers, applying them to naturalised citizens engaged in extremism and making the procedures simpler and more effective.

5. Cases such as Rashid Ramda wanted for the Paris metro bombing 10 years ago and who is still in the UK whilst France seeks extradition, are completely unacceptable. We will begin consultation, on setting a maximum time limit for all future extradition cases involving terrorism.

6. We are already examining a new court procedure which would allow a pre-trial process. We will also examine whether the necessary procedure can be brought about to give us a way of meeting the police and security service request that detention pre-charge of terrorist suspects be significantly extended.

7. For those who are British nationals and who cannot be deported, we will extend the use of control orders. Any breach can mean imprisonment.

8.   To expand the court capacity necessary to deal with this and other related issues, the Lord Chancellor will increase the number of special judges hearing such cases.

9.   We will proscribe Hizb-ut-Tahrir and the successor organisation of Al Muhajiroun. We will also examine the grounds of proscription to widen them and put proposals forward in the new legislation.

10.   It is now necessary, in order to acquire British citizenship, that people attend a citizenship ceremony, swear allegiance to the country and have a rudimentary grasp of the English language. We will review the threshold for this to make sure it is adequate and we will establish, with the Muslim community, a commission to advise on how, consistent with people's complete freedom to worship in the way they want, and to follow their own religion and culture, there is better integration of those parts of the community presently inadequately integrated. I have asked Hazel Blears to make this part of the work she is currently undertaking.

11.   We will consult on a new power to order closure of a place of worship which is used as a centre for fomenting extremism and will consult with Muslim leaders in respect of those clerics who are not British citizens, to draw up a list of those not suitable to preach who will be excluded from Britain.

12.   We will bring forward the proposed measures on the security of our borders, with a series of countries specifically designated for biometric visas over the next year. Meanwhile, the Home Office and Foreign and Commonwealth Office are compiling an international database of those individuals whose activities or views pose a threat to Britain's security. Anyone on the database will be excluded from entry with any appeal only taking place outside the country.

We will consult widely on these measures, including the other political parties of course. This is evidently a heavy agenda to take forward. But it is necessary. Let me also make it clear. If legislation can be made ready in time and the right consensus is achieved, we are ready to recall parliament in September, at least to begin the debate over the measures.

I want to make it clear, yet again, that this is not in any way whatever aimed at the decent, law-abiding Muslim community of Britain. We know this fringe does not truly represent Islam. We know British Muslims in general abhor the actions of the extremists. We acknowledge, once again, Muslim contribution to our country and welcome it; welcome those who visit in peace; welcome those who know that in this country, the respect and tolerance towards others, which we believe in, is the surest guarantee of freedom and progress for people of all religious faiths.

But, coming to Britain is not a right. And even when people have come here, staying here carries with it a duty. That duty is to share and support the values that sustain the British way of life. Those that break that duty and try to incite hatred or engage in violence against our country and its people, have no place here. Over the coming months, in the courts, in parliament, in debate and engagement with all parts of our communities, we will work to turn those sentiments into reality. That is my duty as prime minister.